Working For
Your Dreams

THE COMPLETE
Guide to

AFFILIATE
MARKETING

M L Rusesak

Trient Press
3375 S Rainbow Blvd
#81710, SMB 13135
Las Vegas,NV 89180

Ordering Information:
Quantity sales. Special discounts are available on quantity purchases by corporations, associations, and others. For details, contact the publisher at the address above.
Orders by U.S. trade bookstores and wholesalers. Please contact Trient Press: Tel: (775) 996-3844; or visit www.trientpress.com.

Printed in the United States of America

Publisher's Cataloging-in-Publication data
Ruscsak, M.L.
A title of a book :Working for Your Dreams: The Complete Guide to Affiliate Marketing
ISBN
Paperback   978-1-955198-92-9
E-book   978-1-955198-93-6

PART 1:
INTRODUCTION INTO AFFILIATE MARKETING

CHAPTER 1:

The Basics
Synopsis

Are you tired of working hard in your home business with no real success to show for it? Do you feel like giving up, despite your strong determination to make it work? If so, you're not alone. Many home business owners face the same struggles, but there is hope.

It's a common misconception that success in home businesses is impossible to achieve, but that simply isn't true. In fact, there are numerous ways to find success in today's diverse home business landscape. Whether you've been with your company for a short time or are just starting out, this book is here to help you.

Don't become just another statistic in the alarming trend of home business owners giving up within six months. Instead, take control of your future and join the growing ranks of successful home business owners. This book will guide you on your journey to success, offering practical tips and strategies to help you reach your goals.

The Beginning

Gone are the days of the traditional 9-5 job and the supposed security that comes with working for a large corporation. Society is changing, and people are valuing their time with loved ones and their own personal growth over long commutes and working for someone else.

However, starting a successful business of your own is not a straightforward feat. Statistics show that the majority of such ventures don't make it.

So why do most network marketing businesses fail? Oftentimes, it's due to a lack of proper training and experience. But the industry is now gaining credibility and recognition as a legitimate business model, with many successful entrepreneurs and business people endorsing it.

While network marketing may not be easy, the internet has made it possible to reach a wider range of potential prospects and clients from all over the world. In fact, building business relationships online can be even stronger than offline, as you are able to attract individuals with similar interests, goals, and values.

However, success in network marketing requires hard work and dedication. There's a big difference between a good idea and a successful one that can withstand the pressures of the real world. You can't afford to be weak, lazy, or complacent in this industry – otherwise, your business will fail.

Some may see the risk involved in running a business as daunting, but it's precisely this risk that helps you grow and develop. An entrepreneur who shies away from risk is like a weightlifter who avoids weights.

Embrace the challenge and take the risk to learn something new. With the right tools and mindset, you can achieve success in network marketing..

Get the tools and insight you need to make your business a success.

CHAPTER 2: CREATING YOUR ROAD TO SUCCESS IN NETWORK MARKETING

◆ Overview of network marketing and what it takes to be successful

◆ Produce A Realistic Outlook

◆ Which are your vital principles?

◆ Setting goals and creating a roadmap to success

◆ Understanding the importance of consistency and hard work

In network marketing, success does not come easily. It requires a combination of factors such as hard work, consistency, and a clear understanding of your goals and roadmap to success.

Chapter 2, "Creating Your Road to Success In Network Marketing," provides a comprehensive overview of what it takes to succeed in this industry. From setting achievable goals to the importance of consistency and hard work, this chapter covers everything you need to know to get started on the path to success.

You'll learn about the challenges that come with running your own business, and how to overcome them. The world of network marketing can be relentless, but with the right mindset and the tools to succeed, you can achieve great things.

So, if you're ready to dive into the exciting world of network marketing and start creating your road to success, let's get started!

Produce A Realistic Outlook

Are you ready to turn your network marketing aspirations into a reality? To make that happen, it's crucial to have a clear understanding of what you hope to achieve and why. Whether you're looking to supplement your income, replace your full-time job, or earn a few extra hundred dollars each month, it's important to set a realistic goal and develop a plan to reach it.

To start, take some time to think about what level of income would make you consider your network marketing business a success. This will be the first step in creating a roadmap to achieve your financial aspirations. If your goal is to earn $10,000 a month in the next few years, for example, your plan will need to be much more stringent than if your goal is a few hundred dollars a month.

But money isn't enough. It's important to also identify your motivations for getting involved in network marketing. Knowing why you're working towards a certain level of income will help you stay motivated and focused on your goals, even when the going gets tough.

So, take a deep breath and take the time to determine what level of income you need, and why you're pursuing network marketing. This will set you on the path towards creating a successful and sustainable business.

Answer these questions:
Four years from now, how much monthly income would your company have to make for you to think you are a success?

_____

What are your best ten reasons for doing Network Marketing?
- _____
- _____
- _____
- _____

- _____
- _____
- _____
- _____
- _____
- _____

Now, let's reflect on what motivates you. What drives you to succeed and reach your goals? By understanding your motivations, you can create a powerful vision that will fuel your journey towards success in network marketing.

Are you content with your current job and lifestyle? If so, then your plan might be to supplement your income with network marketing. However, if you're looking to drastically transform your life and live the life of your dreams, then your approach will be quite different.

Having a vision that aligns with your values and positive outlook is crucial for staying motivated and driven. Take the time to visualize what success looks like for you and what steps you need to take to get there. This will keep you motivated, focused and on track towards achieving your goals in network marketing.

Which are your vital principles?

It's time to dig deep and reflect on your core values and beliefs. What drives you and motivates you to succeed? These are your vital principles, and they should always be at the forefront of your mind as you build your network marketing business.

Your vision for your future must align with these principles, and your positive thinking must support them. If you visualize a future that conflicts with your values, you're setting yourself up for self-sabotage. Your mind will say, "Why work so hard if it's not going to be worth it?" and you'll find excuses for not putting in the effort required for success.

But, if you see your future as aligned with your current reality, you'll only have enough self-motivation to achieve what you already have. When the going gets tough, you'll fall back on old habits and remain in the same place.

Take a moment to assess your current vision for the future. Is it positive, negative, or neutral? No matter where you are now, you have the power to create a future that is empowering and inspiring.

Write down your vision and make it as vivid and real as possible. Write it in the first person, present tense, to give it more power and make it feel like it's already happened. "I am now...I have...I am doing...I am contributing to..." and so on. This will help you stay motivated and focused on your goals as you navigate the ups and downs of building your network marketing business.

Don't use pessimistic words. Write as many sensory references as you can as well. What are you experiencing psychologically?

_____

_____

_____

_____

_____

_____

_____

_____

_____

_____

What sights, sounds and smells are currently in the scene you are visualizing? Who are other people there?

_____

_____

_____

_____

_____

_____

_____

_____

_____

_____

_____

Setting Goals and Creating a Roadmap to Success in Network Marketing

The key to success in any endeavor, including network marketing, is to set achievable and measurable goals. Goals provide a sense of direction and motivation and help to focus your efforts in the right direction. By setting goals, you can track your progress and adjust your strategy as needed.

Step 1: Determine your why

Before you start setting goals, it's important to determine your reason for starting a network marketing business. This could be to supplement your income, replace your current job, or simply to have more free time. Whatever your motivation is, it's crucial to understand why you want to succeed in network marketing.

Step 2: Define your goals

Once you have determined your why, it's time to set your goals. Your goals should be specific, measurable, achievable, relevant, and time-bound (SMART). This means that they should be clear and defined, with a deadline for completion. For example, a SMART goal could be "to increase my monthly income from network marketing by $1000 in the next 6 months."

Step 3: Create a roadmap

A roadmap is a visual representation of the steps you need to take to achieve your goals. It should be simple, straightforward, and easy to follow. Your roadmap should include milestones and key actions that will help you achieve your goals.

Step 4: Make a plan

With your roadmap in hand, it's time to make a plan. This should include the tasks you need to complete, the resources you need, and the timeline for each task. Be sure to include both short-term and long-term tasks to keep yourself on track.

Step 5: Track your progress

Tracking your progress is an important part of goal-setting and achieving success in network marketing. Keep a record of your accomplishments, and regularly review your roadmap and plan to see what you have achieved and what still needs to be done.

Step 6: Celebrate your successes

Finally, don't forget to celebrate your successes along the way. Achieving your goals takes hard work and dedication, so take the time to recognize your accomplishments and reward yourself for your efforts.

Setting goals and creating a roadmap to success is essential for anyone looking to build a successful network marketing business. By following these steps, you can ensure that you stay focused, motivated, and on track towards achieving your dreams. With hard work and determination, you can achieve anything you set your mind to in network marketing.

Understanding the Importance of Consistency and Hard Work

In order to be successful in network marketing, it is essential to understand the importance of consistency and hard work. Building a successful network marketing business requires patience, discipline, and a long-term vision. Without consistency and hard work, it will be difficult to achieve your goals and establish a stable, sustainable business.

Consistency is key in network marketing, as success is often a slow process that requires a consistent effort over a long period of time. Whether you are trying to build your network, improve your sales skills, or create a strong brand, it is important to be consistent in your actions and efforts.

Success in network marketing requires a lot of hard work, including the determination to learn and improve, the drive to succeed, and the ability to overcome obstacles. No matter how talented or skilled you are, success will only come through consistent and persistent effort.

Many people get discouraged in network marketing because they do not see immediate results from their efforts. It is important to remember that success in this field is a marathon, not a sprint. It takes time to build a strong and sustainable business, and the rewards of success are well worth the effort.

It is also important to understand that success in network marketing is not a one-man show. Collaborating with other successful network marketers and forming partnerships can help you grow your business and reach your goals faster.

In conclusion, understanding the importance of consistency and hard work is crucial in achieving success in network marketing. By approaching this business with a long-term vision and a commitment to hard work and consistency, you can achieve your goals and build a successful network marketing business.

Setting SMART goals: Set specific, measurable, attainable, relevant, and time-bound goals for their business. This will help them stay focused and motivated.

Creating a vision board: Encourage readers to create a vision board that represents their goals and aspirations in network marketing. They can include images and quotes that inspire them, as well as their business plan and roadmap to success.

Making a plan: Encourage readers to create a detailed plan of action, outlining their steps towards success in network marketing. This plan should include specific tasks, deadlines, and milestones.

Keeping a journal: Encourage readers to keep a journal of their progress and experiences in network marketing. This will help them reflect on what works and what doesn't and make necessary adjustments to their plan.

Staying consistent: Encourage readers to stay consistent in their efforts and actions, even when faced with challenges. Consistency is key to success in network marketing, and it requires hard work and perseverance.

Building a support system: Encourage readers to build a strong support system of friends, family, and other network marketers who can offer advice, encouragement, and support as they pursue their goals.

CHAPTER 3: PLAN YOUR ACHIEVEMENT DIRECTION

The Reality
Let look a bit more in detail.
Understanding your target audience and niche
Developing a marketing plan and strategy
Creating a budget and tracking your progress

Charting Your Path to Success

The Path Ahead
It's time to take a closer look at the roadmap to success.

In this chapter, we will delve into the crucial elements that will set you on the right track towards achieving your goals. From understanding your target audience and niche, to developing a marketing plan and strategy, to creating a budget and tracking your progress, you'll gain a clear understanding of the steps you need to take to succeed in your network marketing business.

The journey to success starts with self-awareness and understanding your strengths and weaknesses. This knowledge will guide you in developing a plan that matches your aspirations and is tailored to your unique skills and abilities.

The truth is, no matter what type of business you start, success requires hard work and effort. Don't be misled by the idea that you can simply push a button and the money will come pouring in. The road to success is paved with perseverance, dedication, and the willingness to learn and grow.

Whether you have existing skills and talent, or you need to invest in training and education, it's important to acknowledge that your business will require effort and investment. So, let's take an honest look at the path to success and get started on your journey today!

The Reality

Welcome to the reality of the entrepreneurial journey! So, you have a dream of running a successful business, and that's great! But before you jump into the deep end, let's take a step back and have an honest look at what it takes to get there.

Contrary to popular belief, running a business isn't as simple as pushing a button and watching the money roll in. Whether it's writing articles to promote affiliate products or selling handmade crafts, every business requires effort and a certain set of skills.

Let's take a look at what's involved in running a simple marketing business. Writing, for starters, is a key component, and not everyone has the writing skills to succeed in this field. And even if you're a great writer, there's more to it than that. You also need to know how to do keyword research, niche research, and find products that have proven to sell.

But even if you have the skills, there's still another crucial element that makes the difference between success and failure: work ethic. Some people just don't have the drive to do what it takes to make it in network marketing. They see how much work is involved, and they quit. This is why you'll often hear the phrase "working smarter, not harder."

The truth is, making money online is hard work. If it was easy, everyone would be doing it. But don't let this discourage you! With the right training, discipline, and a solid work ethic, you can achieve great things.

So, it's time to start building the foundation for your success. Start developing the skills you need, and be prepared to put in the effort to make your dreams a reality. The journey ahead may not be easy, but with determination and persistence, you'll get there!

Logically, the basis of any business plan will have three common elements:
Goods and services:

1. Understand your company's goods or services. Compare your own company's goods over those offered by all rivals, and scrutinize your own business. Become familiar with all your products and the unique features that make them so much better than others. Develop a true belief in the value of the goods.

2. Talk about your goods or services with others on a daily basis. Keep a list of buyers who may benefit from your company's goods. As you go about your day, watch for chances to suggest your goods to those whom may have a need for them.

In network marketing, getting buyers comes by introducing other people to some of the benefits your business offers.

3. Support the individuals in your company who see the importance of producing a home based income that might add to their lives.

Let look a bit more in detail.

Plan Your Achievement Direction - Understanding Your Target Audience and Niche

As you embark on your journey to success in network marketing, it is important to understand the importance of knowing your target audience and finding your niche. You want to ensure that the products or services you offer are of the highest quality and are exactly what your potential customers are looking for. To do this, you need to have a deep understanding of the products and what makes them special and valuable to your target audience.

One of the first things you should do is talk to people in your network marketing business and your upline to get their perspectives on each product and why they believe it is exceptional. This will give you valuable insights into the products and can help you determine what makes them stand out from your competitors.

Additionally, you should take the time to learn about all the uses for each product and identify any groups or markets that may have a particular benefit from them. This will help you focus your prospecting efforts on these groups and tailor your marketing efforts and special offers to their specific needs and interests.

To succeed in network marketing, it is also important to have the right tools and training in place. This will allow you to effectively reach your target audience, understand their needs, and build relationships with them. A professional network marketer should always be constantly learning and seeking out new training opportunities to stay ahead of the game and provide the best products and services to their customers.

Understanding your target audience and finding your niche is a critical component of success in network marketing. By taking the time to get to know your customers and their needs, you can create a marketing plan and strategy that will help you achieve your goals and reach new heights of success.

It is essential for those just beginning to be cognizant of some basics required, which include:

Affordable Long-Distance Plan: Choose a plan that charges you less than $0.05 per minute for long-distance calls. If you frequently make long-distance calls, opt for an unlimited calling plan to save money.

Conference and Three-Party Calling: Call your provider to set up conference or three-party calling, which is useful for connecting with prospects and team members for demonstrations and training.

Professional Voice Mail: Invest in voice mail instead of using an outdated answering machine. Record a professional message that greets callers with a warm and welcoming first impression.

Consider getting a toll-free contact number to encourage prospects to call you back.

If you conduct business from various locations, a mobile phone can be handy. Choose a plan that fits your needs.

Set up a checking account specifically for your network marketing business and keep records of all expenses. You can use a net checkbook or database software to enter monthly payment details, making it easier to track expenses and calculate taxes.

In today's tech-savvy world, a computer or laptop is a must. Use it to communicate with buyers, team members, leads, and the company via email, write letters, and market your products or services.

Business cards and other communication materials are important for presenting yourself as a professional. Consider adding a personalized company logo for a more professional touch.

If your company offers an automatic shipping program, sign up for it. Not only will you receive regular deliveries of your products, but you'll also set a good example for your team and ensure you never miss a commission check by forgetting to order products.

Set up a duplicable website: Your website can be a low-cost way to acquire leads and showcase your business offerings, and also serve as an example for your team.

Prepare materials: If you sell retail goods, order business catalogues, prospecting booklets, or audio tapes. Have packages ready at all times so you don't miss a good prospecting opportunity.

Learn about the company: Study the materials provided by the company, including the pay plan, so you can share its best points with enthusiasm.

Utilize pre-recorded calls: If the company or your upline offers pre-recorded opportunity calls, take advantage and set up three-party calls. If not, work with your team to create one.

Get support from upline leaders: Get the names and numbers of all your upline leaders. They benefit from your work, so take advantage of their support.

Create a story letter: Write a letter introducing people to your business, products, and opportunity. Explain how you became involved with the company and why you chose to pursue a home-based income opportunity.

It is now time for us to talk about the numbers of network marketing. Speaking with enough people to fill your pipeline with a ceaseless stream of interested leads is vital to accomplishing success.

Understanding Your Target Audience and Niche

When it comes to building a successful business, it's important to understand who your target audience is and what their needs are. Your target audience refers to the group of people who are most likely to purchase your products or services. Knowing your target audience and what they're looking for can help you create a more effective marketing strategy and increase your chances of success.

One of the first steps in understanding your target audience is to define your niche. A niche is a specific segment of the market that you can focus on to gain a competitive advantage. A niche can be based on a variety of factors, including age, gender, location, interests, and more.

Once you've defined your niche, it's important to conduct market research to gain a deeper understanding of your target audience. This can involve surveying current and potential customers, analyzing data from your website and social media channels, and studying trends and patterns in your industry.

One useful tool for conducting market research is a buyer persona. A buyer persona is a fictional representation of your ideal customer, based on data and research. By creating a buyer persona, you can gain a better understanding of your target audience and what their needs and pain points are.

Once you have a solid understanding of your target audience and niche, you can start to tailor your marketing efforts to meet their needs. This can involve creating targeted content, adjusting your pricing strategy, and offering promotions and discounts that are specifically designed to appeal to your target audience.

It's also important to continually monitor and analyze your target audience and niche to ensure that your marketing efforts are still aligned with their needs and preferences. As your business grows and evolves, your target audience and niche may also change, so it's important to stay up-to-date and make adjustments as needed.

Understanding your target audience and niche is crucial for building a successful business. By taking the time to research and understand your target audience, you can create a more effective marketing strategy and increase your chances of success

Developing a Marketing Plan and Strategy

Marketing is an essential component of any successful business, and it is crucial to develop a well-structured marketing plan to reach your target audience effectively. A marketing plan defines your target audience, sets goals and objectives, and outlines the strategies and tactics you will use to reach your goals. This chapter will help you understand how to create a marketing plan and strategy to promote your network marketing business effectively.

Define Your Target Audience

The first step in developing your marketing plan is to identify your target audience. Who are the people most likely to be interested in your products or services? What are their needs and wants? What motivates them to make a purchase? Understanding your target audience is critical to creating an effective marketing strategy. You can gather information about your target audience through market research, surveys, and customer data analysis.

Set Your Goals and Objectives

Once you have identified your target audience, it is time to set your marketing goals and objectives. These should be specific, measurable, achievable, relevant, and time-bound (SMART). For example, your goal may be to increase website traffic by 25% in the next six months, or to generate 100 new leads per month through social media marketing. Your objectives should support your goals and be specific enough to track progress and measure success.

Identify Your Unique Selling Proposition (USP)

Your Unique Selling Proposition (USP) is what sets you apart from your competitors. What makes your products or services different and why should people choose you over others? Identifying your USP is critical to developing a successful marketing strategy and messaging.

Choose Your Marketing Channels

Once you have defined your target audience, set your goals and objectives, and identified your USP, it's time to choose the marketing channels that will best reach your target audience. There are many marketing channels to choose from, including social media, email marketing, content marketing, search engine optimization, and more. Consider which channels will reach your target audience most effectively and allocate your budget accordingly.

Develop Your Marketing Mix

The marketing mix is a combination of the four P's: product, price, place, and promotion. To develop your marketing mix, consider how you will position your product or service, what price you will charge, where you will sell it, and how you will promote it.

Create Your Marketing Budget

Finally, you need to create a marketing budget that outlines how much money you will spend on each marketing channel and the resources you will allocate to each. Your marketing budget should be realistic, based on your goals and objectives, and should consider the cost of any necessary tools or services.

Monitor and Evaluate Your Results

It's important to monitor and evaluate the results of your marketing plan and make adjustments as necessary. Regularly review your metrics and KPIs to measure your success and make changes to your strategy if needed. This will help you stay on track and reach your goals.

In conclusion, developing a marketing plan and strategy is an essential step in promoting your network marketing business effectively. By defining your target audience, setting goals and objectives, choosing marketing channels, developing your marketing mix, creating a budget, and monitoring and evaluating your results, you will have a roadmap for success.

Sample Marketing Plan

Developing a Marketing Plan and Strategy for an Affiliate and MLM Business

Marketing is a crucial aspect of any business. It is the process of creating awareness of your products, services, and business opportunities to your target audience. A marketing plan outlines your strategy for attracting and retaining customers, and reaching your business goals. An effective marketing plan should take into account the target audience, market trends, competition, and budget. In this chapter, we will outline a sample marketing plan and strategy for an affiliate and MLM business.

Target Audience

The first step in developing a marketing plan and strategy is to understand your target audience. Your target audience should be specific, measurable, attainable, relevant, and time-bound (SMART). Consider the following when defining your target audience:

Demographics: Age, gender, income, education level, location, etc.
Interests: Hobbies, passions, lifestyles, etc.
Needs: Products or services that can solve a problem or fulfill a desire.
For our sample marketing plan, let's assume that the target audience is health-conscious individuals aged 25-55, who are interested in wellness, fitness, and natural health solutions. They are looking for products that can help improve their overall health, boost energy levels, and support a healthy lifestyle.

Marketing Channels

Once you have defined your target audience, the next step is to determine the marketing channels you will use to reach them. Consider the following:

- ✧ **Social Media:** Facebook, Instagram, Twitter, etc.
- ✧ **Content Marketing:** Blogs, articles, videos, etc.
- ✧ **Email Marketing:** Newsletters, promotional emails, etc.
- ✧ **Affiliate Marketing:** Partnering with other businesses to promote your products and services.
- ✧ **MLM:** Leveraging a network of independent distributors to promote your products and services.
- ✧ For our sample marketing plan, we will use a combination of social media, content marketing, and email marketing to reach our target audience. We will also leverage affiliate marketing and MLM to expand our reach and reach new customers.

Marketing Budget

The next step is to determine your marketing budget. Your marketing budget should be a percentage of your overall revenue and should reflect your marketing goals and strategies. Consider the following when determining your marketing budget:

Marketing channels: The cost of each marketing channel, including advertising, content creation, and distribution.

Marketing materials: The cost of creating and distributing marketing materials, including brochures, flyers, and business cards.

Marketing software: The cost of marketing software, including email marketing software, CRM software, and social media management tools.

For our sample marketing plan, we will allocate a marketing budget of 10% of our overall revenue. This budget will be used to create and distribute marketing materials, run social media campaigns, and leverage affiliate and MLM marketing.

Marketing Strategy

The final step in developing a marketing plan and strategy is to outline your marketing strategy. Consider the following when developing your marketing strategy:

Brand Awareness: Create awareness of your brand and products through social media, content marketing, and email marketing.

Lead Generation: Generate leads through targeted social media campaigns, content marketing, and email marketing.

Conversion: Convert leads into customers through targeted email campaigns, follow-up calls, and in-person demonstrations.

Retention: Retain customers through regular engagement and customer loyalty programs.

For our sample marketing plan, we will focus on brand awareness, lead generation, conversion, and retention. Our strategy will include the following:

Social Media Campaigns: We will run targeted social media campaigns on platforms such as Facebook, Instagram, and Twitter to reach a larger audience and increase brand awareness. Our campaigns will be aimed at people who are interested in home-based business opportunities, network marketing, and personal development. We will use visually appealing graphics, engaging content, and relevant hashtags to make our posts stand out and drive engagement. Our goal is to reach 10,000 people and generate 500 leads in the first quarter.

Content Marketing: To establish our brand as a thought leader in the home-based business and network marketing space, we will create and distribute valuable and informative content through blog posts, videos, infographics, and email newsletters. Our content will address common challenges faced by entrepreneurs, highlight success stories of our affiliates, and educate people about the benefits of our products and opportunity. We will also collaborate with influencers and bloggers in our niche to reach a wider audience.

Referral Marketing: Our affiliates are our biggest brand ambassadors and we will incentivize them to refer their friends and family to our business by offering rewards and bonuses. We will also provide them with training, tools, and resources to help them effectively promote our products and opportunity.

Event Marketing: We will organize local events and workshops to engage with our existing affiliates and reach out to new prospects. These events will provide an opportunity for our affiliates to meet one another, learn new skills, and hear from successful entrepreneurs in our company.

Search Engine Optimization: We will optimize our website and blog content to rank higher in search engines and drive organic traffic. Our focus will be on using relevant keywords, creating high-quality content, and building quality backlinks.

Overall, our marketing plan and strategy will focus on building a strong online presence, educating our target audience, and engaging with our affiliates and prospects. By executing this plan consistently, we aim to increase brand awareness, drive traffic, generate leads, and ultimately, grow our business.

Creating a Budget and Tracking Your Progress

A budget is a crucial aspect of any marketing plan and strategy, regardless of whether it is for an affiliate or multi-level marketing (MLM) business. The budget helps to ensure that your marketing efforts are supported by a realistic allocation of resources, and it helps you track your progress towards achieving your marketing goals. In this chapter, we will discuss the key components of a marketing budget and how to create one for your business. We will also discuss the importance of tracking your progress and how to do it effectively.

Key Components of a Marketing Budget

A marketing budget typically includes the following components:

Advertising and Promotion: This includes the cost of running advertisements, such as online ads, print ads, or television commercials, as well as the cost of promoting your products or services through events, sponsorships, or influencer marketing campaigns.

Market Research: This includes the cost of conducting market research to understand your target audience, their needs and preferences, and the competitive landscape.

Content Creation: This includes the cost of creating and producing marketing materials such as blog posts, videos, images, or e-books.

Social Media Management: This includes the cost of managing your social media accounts, such as hiring a social media manager, paying for social media tools, and advertising on social media platforms.

Website Development: This includes the cost of designing and developing your website, as well as any ongoing website maintenance and updates.

Lead Generation: This includes the cost of generating leads, such as through email campaigns, webinars, or paid search campaigns.

Sales and Support: This includes the cost of sales and support activities, such as hiring a sales team, providing customer support, or offering product demonstrations.

Creating a Marketing Budget

To create a marketing budget, you will need to start by setting your marketing goals and determining the resources that you will need to achieve them. This includes considering the costs of each of the components listed above, as well as any other expenses related to your marketing activities. Once you have an estimate of the resources that you will need, you can create a budget by allocating funds to each of the components of your marketing plan.

It is important to note that a marketing budget is not a one-time expense. Your budget should be updated regularly to reflect changes in your marketing goals and strategies, as well as changes in market conditions or other external factors.

Tracking Your Progress

Tracking your progress is an important part of any marketing plan and strategy. By monitoring your progress, you can identify areas where your marketing efforts are succeeding, as well as areas that may need improvement. You can then make adjustments to your marketing plan and budget as needed to maximize your results.

To track your progress, you will need to establish key performance indicators (KPIs) that are specific, measurable, and relevant to your marketing goals. Some common KPIs for tracking marketing progress include website traffic, lead generation, conversion rates, and customer satisfaction. You can use a variety of tools to track your KPIs, such as Google Analytics, marketing automation software, or a spreadsheet.

Creating a budget and tracking your progress are essential components of any marketing plan and strategy. By following a structured process and using the right tools, you can ensure that your marketing efforts are supported by a realistic budget, and that you are able to track your progress towards achieving your marketing goals.

Conclusion

In this chapter, we discussed the importance of developing a comprehensive marketing plan and strategy, understanding your target audience and niche, and creating a budget and tracking your progress. All these elements are crucial in ensuring the success of any business, particularly in affiliate and MLM marketing.

A well-defined marketing plan and strategy can help you to identify your target audience, reach them effectively, and communicate the value of your products or services. This can increase the chances of attracting and retaining customers, and ultimately drive sales and revenue. Understanding your target audience and niche will allow you to create a more relevant and appealing marketing message, while creating a budget and tracking your progress will help you to stay on track and measure the effectiveness of your marketing efforts.

Social media campaigns, email marketing, and influencer marketing were among the key marketing channels discussed in this chapter. By effectively utilizing these channels, businesses can reach their target audience, build brand awareness, and drive sales.

In conclusion, creating a comprehensive marketing plan and strategy, understanding your target audience and niche, and creating a budget and tracking your progress are essential steps in ensuring the success of an affiliate or MLM business. It is important to continually analyze, refine, and adjust your marketing efforts to achieve your desired results. With a well-planned and executed marketing plan, businesses can increase their chances of success and growth in the highly competitive world of affiliate and MLM marketing.

CHAPTER 4: METHODS TO FIND POTENTIAL PROSPECTS

Identifying your ideal customer
Building a prospect list and nurturing your leads
Utilizing various methods to find potential prospects, such as online and offline methods

Methods to Find Potential Prospects

In the world of network marketing, success depends on two things: having a great product to offer and finding people to offer it to. Without a steady stream of prospects, even the best products will fail to generate sales and profits. That's why it's important to understand the various methods to find potential prospects and turn them into loyal customers.

In this chapter, we will explore the key methods to find potential prospects and help you get the most out of your marketing efforts. First, we will discuss the importance of identifying your ideal customer. This will help you understand who you should be targeting and how to reach them. Next, we will explore the process of building a prospect list and nurturing your leads. This is an essential step to keeping your business growing and ensuring long-term success.

We will then dive into the various methods to find potential prospects, including online and offline methods. These will include techniques such as social media marketing, email marketing, and even old-fashioned face-to-face networking. The goal is to help you understand how to make the most of each method, so you can reach your ideal customers and keep your business growing.

Motivate the Spectators Throughout

In network marketing, success often depends on the ability to motivate others. Whether it's your team, your prospects, or your customers, it's essential to keep everyone motivated and engaged. In this chapter, we will explore the methods you can use to motivate the people around you and help keep your business growing.

We will discuss the importance of having a clear vision and mission, and how this can help you and your team stay motivated and focused. We will also explore the role of incentives, rewards, and recognition in motivating others. We will look at how you can use these tools to inspire and engage your prospects and customers, and how to build a culture of motivation and success within your business.

In conclusion, this chapter will provide you with the knowledge and tools you need to motivate the people around you and keep your business growing. Whether you're working with your team, prospects, or customers, these methods will help you create a culture of motivation and success, and ensure long-term success for your business.

Identifying your ideal customer

Knowing who your ideal customer is one of the most important aspects of your network marketing and affiliate marketing business. Your ideal customer will be the person who will be most interested in what you have to offer, making it easier for you to connect with them, engage with them and sell your products or services to them. In this chapter, we will discuss the steps you need to take to identify your ideal customer, including the following:

Define your target market
Before you can identify your ideal customer, you need to know who your target market is. Your target market is a group of people who share similar characteristics, such as age, income, location, interests, and needs. Once you

know who your target market is, you can begin to identify the specific characteristics of your ideal customer.

Identify your customer's pain points
One of the most effective ways to identify your ideal customer is to understand what problems they face. What are the pain points that your products or services can help solve? This information will help you to develop a marketing message that speaks directly to your customer's needs and addresses their pain points.

Determine your customer's buying habits
Knowing your customer's buying habits is important when identifying your ideal customer. Do they prefer to buy online or in-store? Do they like to receive promotions or discounts? What motivates them to make a purchase? Understanding your customer's buying habits will help you to create marketing campaigns that resonate with them and increase the chances of them making a purchase.

Create a customer profile
Once you have gathered all of the information about your ideal customer, you can create a customer profile. A customer profile is a detailed description of your ideal customer, including their demographics, interests, pain points, and buying habits. This profile will be a valuable tool in helping you to create marketing campaigns that resonate with your ideal customer.

By taking the time to identify your ideal customer, you can create marketing campaigns that will speak directly to their needs and interests, increasing the chances of them becoming a customer. The more you understand your ideal customer, the more effective your marketing campaigns will be, leading to increased sales and profits.

Building a Prospect List and Nurturing Your Leads

Once you have identified your ideal customer, it's time to focus on building a prospect list and nurturing your leads. Your prospect list will consist of individuals who are interested in your product or service and who have the potential to become customers. Nurturing your leads involves developing a relationship with them, so that they are more likely to become customers in the future.

Building a Prospect List

Gather Information: To build your prospect list, gather information about your ideal customer, such as their name, address, email, and phone number. You can gather this information through a variety of sources, such as your company's database, trade shows, surveys, and social media.

Segment Your List: Once you have gathered information about your ideal customer, it's time to segment your list. This involves dividing your list into groups based on common characteristics, such as age, location, and buying habits. Segmenting your list will help you to tailor your marketing messages and offers to specific groups of individuals, which will increase their effectiveness.

Keep Your List Up-to-Date: It's important to keep your prospect list up-to-date. This involves regularly removing individuals who are no longer interested in your product or service and adding new individuals to your list.

Nurturing Your Leads

Build Relationships: Nurturing your leads involves building relationships with individuals on your prospect list. This can be achieved through regular communication, such as email newsletters, phone calls, and personal follow-ups.

Provide Value: To build relationships with your leads, it's important to provide them with value. This can include educational materials, such as white papers, e-books, and webinars, that will help them to make informed decisions about your product or service.

Stay in Touch: Regular communication with your leads will help to keep them interested in your product or service. This can include regular email newsletters, phone calls, and personal follow-ups.

Building a prospect list and nurturing your leads is an important part of growing your business. By gathering information about your ideal customer and regularly communicating with your leads, you can build strong relationships and increase the likelihood of them becoming customers in the future. By following the steps outlined in this chapter, you can build a successful prospect list and nurture your leads, leading to increased growth and success for your business.

Utilizing Various Methods to Find Potential Prospects

When it comes to finding potential prospects, there are a variety of methods available, both online and offline. In order to be successful in building a large and interested prospect list, it is important to utilize a combination of these methods. Here are a few tips to help you get started.

Online Methods:

Social Media: Social media is a powerful tool for finding potential prospects. Utilize platforms like Facebook, Instagram, and LinkedIn to connect with people in your target audience and build relationships with them. Share valuable content, participate in online communities, and engage with your followers to build trust and establish yourself as a subject matter expert in your niche.

Website Optimization: Optimize your website for search engines to increase your visibility and reach potential prospects. Utilize keywords, meta descriptions, and other SEO best practices to ensure that your website is easy to find and relevant to your target audience.

Content Marketing: Creating valuable content can help you attract and engage with potential prospects. Offer blog posts, videos, infographics, and other types of content that provides value to your target audience and positions you as an expert in your niche.

Offline Methods:

Networking: Networking events and industry conferences are great places to meet potential prospects face-to-face. Attend these events and engage in conversations with people in your target audience to build relationships and generate leads.

Referrals: Ask for referrals from current customers, friends, and family members. Your current network can be a valuable resource for finding new prospects.

Direct Mail: Utilize direct mail campaigns to reach potential prospects with targeted and personalized messages. Direct mail campaigns can include postcards, letters, and other physical materials that can be sent directly to a prospect's mailbox.

There are a variety of methods available for finding potential prospects, both online and offline. Utilizing a combination of these methods will help you reach a wider audience and increase your chances of success. Remember to always focus on building relationships and providing value to your prospects, and your efforts will be rewarded with a growing prospect list and increased sales.

Conclusion:

In this chapter, we covered the crucial steps for finding and identifying your ideal customer and building a prospect list to reach them. We emphasized the importance of knowing your target audience and how to create a profile that can help you identify their needs, interests, and behavior patterns. By building a prospect list, you can reach your ideal customer and increase your chances of making a successful sale.

We also discussed the various methods to find potential prospects, both online and offline. From using social media to networking events, there are many ways to reach your target audience and generate leads. By utilizing these methods and testing what works best for your business, you can find and reach your ideal customer.

To summarize, finding and reaching your ideal customer is a crucial step in the success of your business. By identifying your target audience and utilizing various methods to reach them, you can build a successful prospect list and increase your chances of making a sale.

Engagement Questions:

What steps have you taken to identify your ideal customer?
How have you been building your prospect list?
What methods have you found to be most effective for reaching potential prospects?
How do you plan to continue nurturing your leads and keeping them engaged with your business?

CHAPTER 5: MOTIVATE THE SPECTATORS THROUGHOUT - A KEY COMPONENT OF SUCCESS

Building relationships with prospects and customers
Providing value and creating trust
Overcoming objections and closing sales

As you embark on your journey as an affiliate or multi-level marketer, it's critical to understand how to motivate your prospects and turn them into customers. Building strong relationships with your target audience is essential to your success, as it creates trust and establishes you as a valuable resource for information and support. This chapter will focus on strategies for building relationships, providing value, and overcoming objections to close sales and turn prospects into loyal customers.

Whether you are new to affiliate and MLM marketing or have been in the industry for years, this chapter will provide you with the tools and insights you need to effectively motivate your prospects and achieve success. From building relationships with your prospects to providing value, this chapter will guide you through the essential steps to motivating your spectators throughout the sales process. So buckle up, take notes and get ready to take your marketing skills to the next level!

Building Relationships with Prospects and Customers

Building relationships with prospects and customers is the key to success in any MLM or affiliate marketing business. This chapter will explore the importance of developing strong connections with your target audience, and provide you with tips and techniques for nurturing these relationships over time.

The first step in building relationships with your prospects and customers is to get to know them. You need to understand their needs, wants, and challenges, so you can provide them with the products and services that will meet those needs and solve their problems. This requires active listening and empathy, so you can put yourself in their shoes and understand their perspectives.

Another important aspect of building relationships is providing value. You want to establish yourself as a trusted resource and expert in your industry, so that your prospects and customers will turn to you for advice and solutions. You can do this by providing valuable information, such as articles, blog posts, videos, and webinars, that will help your prospects and customers solve their problems and achieve their goals.

In addition to providing value, you also need to create trust. Trust is built over time, through consistent, honest, and transparent interactions with your prospects and customers. You need to be responsive, reliable, and always follow through on your promises. You also need to be willing to admit when you don't know something, and show your willingness to learn and grow.

Finally, it's important to nurture your relationships with your prospects and customers over time. This means staying in touch on a regular basis, following up with them after sales, and continually providing value and building trust. You can use email marketing, direct mail, and social media to stay in touch, and consider hosting events or webinars that your prospects and customers can attend to build deeper relationships.

By building strong relationships with your prospects and customers, you will not only increase sales and conversions, but you will also build a loyal customer base that will become ambassadors for your brand and promote your products and services to others.

Providing Value and Creating Trust

In the world of marketing and sales, building trust with your prospects and customers is essential to long-term success. When people trust you, they are more likely to become loyal customers and recommend your business to others. To build trust, you need to provide value to your prospects and customers, both in the form of high-quality products and services, and in the way you interact with them.

One of the most important ways to provide value is to clearly communicate the benefits of your products and services. This can be done through effective marketing messages and by offering demonstrations or samples. You can also offer a satisfaction guarantee or a free trial period to give your prospects the chance to experience your products and services without risk.

Another way to provide value is by offering helpful information and resources. This can include educational articles, videos, and webinars, as well as personalized advice and support. When you invest time and resources into helping your prospects and customers, you demonstrate your commitment to their success, which in turn builds trust.

It's also important to be transparent and honest in your interactions with prospects and customers. When you make a mistake, admit it and make things right. When you can't provide the solution they are looking for, be upfront and help them find a better alternative. By being transparent and honest, you build credibility and earn the trust of your prospects and customers.

In addition, it's important to provide exceptional customer service. Respond to customer inquiries promptly and professionally, and be proactive in resolving any issues that may arise. By demonstrating a genuine commitment to your customers' satisfaction, you build trust and foster long-term relationships.

In conclusion, providing value and building trust are essential components of any successful marketing and sales strategy. By clearly communicating the benefits of your products and services, offering helpful information and resources, being transparent and honest, and providing exceptional customer service, you can establish a reputation as a trusted and valuable resource in the eyes of your prospects and customers.

Overcoming Objections and Closing Sales

Closing sales is a critical step in the sales process, and it can be challenging if you face objections from your prospects. However, with the right approach, you can overcome objections and successfully close sales. Here are some tips on how to handle objections and close sales effectively.

Understand the Objection

The first step in overcoming objections is to understand the underlying concern behind the objection. Listen to the objection carefully and ask clarifying questions to determine the root cause. For example, if a prospect objects to the price of your product, ask questions to find out why they feel that the price is too high. This will give you the information you need to address the objection effectively.

Provide Relevant Information

Once you understand the objection, provide relevant information to address the concern. For example, if the objection is about the price of your product, you could provide information about the product's value and how it compares to similar products in the market. If the objection is about the product's quality, you could provide testimonials from satisfied customers or data on the product's reliability.

Find a Compromise

If the prospect's objection cannot be completely addressed, look for a compromise. For example, if the prospect objects to the price, you could offer a discount or a flexible payment plan. If the objection is about the product's features, you could suggest alternative products that meet their needs better.

Close the Sale

Finally, once you have addressed the objection, it's time to close the sale. Ask for the prospect's decision and be confident in your product and its benefits. If the prospect is still hesitant, ask if there is anything else that they need to know or consider before making a decision.

In conclusion, overcoming objections and closing sales is an important part of the sales process. By understanding the objection, providing relevant information, finding a compromise, and closing the sale, you can effectively handle objections and successfully close sales.

Engagement Questions:

What are some common objections that you have faced in your sales process?

How do you handle objections effectively?

What strategies have you found to be successful in closing sales?

How do you build trust with prospects and overcome objections at the same time?

Chapter 6: Generating Leads and Prospects Online

Understanding the importance of online marketing for network marketing success

Using social media and other online platforms to reach your target audience

Building an online presence and creating a brand identity

Generating Leads and Prospects Online - The Power of Online Marketing

In today's digital age, having a strong online presence is crucial to the success of any business, including network marketing. The internet provides numerous opportunities to reach a wider audience, build brand recognition, and connect with potential prospects. This chapter will delve into the importance of online marketing for network marketing success, and explore various online platforms and techniques that can help you reach your target audience. From social media to building an online brand identity, you will learn how to effectively use the power of the internet to generate leads and prospects for your network marketing business. So buckle up and get ready to tap into the unlimited potential of online marketing.

Understanding the Importance of Online Marketing for Network Marketing Success

In today's digital age, online marketing has become a crucial aspect of any business, including network marketing. With the rise of the internet, potential customers are more likely to be found online than anywhere else. As a result, having a strong online presence is essential for the success of your network marketing business.

The Importance of Online Marketing for Network Marketing

Online marketing provides an efficient and cost-effective way to reach your target audience. Unlike traditional marketing methods, online marketing allows you to reach a wider audience with less time and effort. You can use social media platforms, email marketing, and other digital marketing strategies to reach your target audience in a matter of minutes.

Another advantage of online marketing is the ability to track and measure your results. You can use analytics tools to see which marketing strategies are working and which are not. This allows you to make data-driven decisions and adjust your marketing plan accordingly.

The Benefits of Online Marketing for Network Marketing

One of the biggest benefits of online marketing is the ability to reach a global audience. With social media platforms, you can reach potential customers from anywhere in the world. This expands your reach and opens up new opportunities for growth.

Online marketing also enables you to build a strong brand identity. By consistently providing value and creating a unique brand voice, you can establish yourself as a leader in your industry. This will help you to attract more customers and increase your visibility online.

Finally, online marketing provides a platform for you to connect with your audience and build relationships. By engaging with your followers on social media, responding to comments and messages, and creating valuable content, you can create a sense of community around your brand. This will help you to build trust and establish yourself as a credible and reliable source of information in your industry.

Online marketing is a crucial aspect of network marketing success. By understanding its importance and utilizing various online platforms, you can reach a wider audience, build your brand, and connect with your target audience. In this chapter, we will explore the different methods of generating leads and prospects online, so that you can make the most of this powerful marketing tool.

Building an Online Presence and Creating a Brand Identity

Creating an online presence is an essential aspect of network marketing success in the digital age. With the rise of technology and the internet, a large portion of the population is spending more and more time online, making it crucial for network marketers to have a strong presence on the web. In this chapter, we will discuss the key steps to building an online presence and creating a brand identity that will help you attract and engage with your target audience.

Establishing your brand identity: A brand identity is a set of visual and verbal elements that defines your company, products, and services. It is crucial to have a strong brand identity because it helps differentiate your business from others and build trust with your target audience. Some important elements to consider when creating your brand identity include your logo, color scheme, font, messaging, and tone of voice.

Building a website: Your website is the cornerstone of your online presence and the primary destination for your target audience. It should be professional, user-friendly, and optimized for search engines. Your website should include key information about your company, products, and services, as well as a blog, contact information, and a call to action.

Utilizing social media: Social media platforms such as Facebook, Twitter, and Instagram are powerful tools for reaching and engaging with your target audience. You should choose the platforms that are most relevant to your audience and post regularly, providing value, and creating engagement. Social media is also a great way to showcase your brand identity and build relationships with your followers.

Creating content: Content creation is an important part of building an online presence and attracting potential customers. Content can come in many forms, including blog posts, videos, infographics, and social media updates. The goal of your content should be to educate and inform your target audience, build trust, and establish your expertise.

Building an online presence and creating a brand identity is essential for network marketing success in the digital age. By following these key steps, you will be able to reach and engage with your target audience, build trust, and establish your expertise. The key to success is to consistently create and share valuable content that resonates with your target audience.

In this chapter, we explored the significance of online marketing for network marketing success. Online marketing provides a vast platform to reach your target audience, build an online presence, and create a brand identity. Utilizing various tools such as social media, email marketing, and content creation, you can effectively promote your business and connect with your audience.

To achieve success in online marketing, it's essential to have a comprehensive understanding of your target audience, their needs and preferences, and the best ways to reach them. Additionally, having a strong online presence through a well-designed website, social media profiles, and high-quality content can help you establish a positive image for your brand and increase your chances of success.

Engagement Questions:

How can you effectively use social media to reach your target audience?
What steps can you take to create a strong online presence for your network marketing business?
How can you create high-quality content that resonates with your target audience and helps build trust?
What are some best practices for maintaining a consistent brand identity across all of your online platforms?

CHAPTER 7: INVOLVEMENT OF INTERNET IN NETWORK MARKETING

Utilizing technology and the internet to automate and scale your network marketing business

Staying up-to-date with the latest tools and strategies for online marketing

Building a team and leveraging the power of collaboration

As we enter the digital age, the role of technology and the internet in business has become increasingly significant. Network marketing is no exception, as it too has been transformed by the power of technology and the internet. In this chapter, we will explore the ways in which technology and the internet can be used to automate and scale your network marketing business. We will also discuss the importance of staying up-to-date with the latest tools and strategies for online marketing, and the benefits of building a team and leveraging the power of collaboration. By the end of this chapter, you will have a better understanding of how technology and the internet can be leveraged to help you achieve success in your network marketing endeavors. So, let's dive in and explore the exciting world of technology and network marketing!

Utilizing Technology and the Internet to Automate and Scale Your Network Marketing Business

In today's world, technology and the internet play a crucial role in the success of a network marketing business. With the advancements in technology, network marketers have the opportunity to automate many of the tasks that once took up valuable time and energy. This automation not only saves time but also helps to scale the business, making it easier to reach more prospects and customers. In this chapter, we will discuss how you can use technology and the internet to automate and scale your network marketing business.

One of the key ways to utilize technology is by implementing automation tools and software. For example, you can use a customer relationship management (CRM) system to manage your contacts and automate your follow-up process. You can also use an email marketing platform to send automated emails to your prospects and customers, which can save time and improve the efficiency of your communication.

Another way to use technology is by leveraging social media and other online platforms to reach your target audience. You can use platforms like Facebook, Twitter, and LinkedIn to connect with your prospects and customers, share your products and services, and build relationships. With social media, you can also automate many of the tasks involved in maintaining your presence, such as scheduling posts and responding to messages.

In addition to automation, technology can also help you to scale your business. For example, you can use video marketing to reach a wider audience and provide value to your prospects and customers. You can also use webinars to connect with your target audience and provide training and education on your products and services.

Technology and the internet play a critical role in the success of a network marketing business. By utilizing automation tools and software, leveraging social media and other online platforms, and using technology to scale your business, you can increase your reach, build stronger relationships with your prospects and customers, and grow your network marketing business.

Engagement Questions
How has technology impacted network marketing in recent years?
What tools and resources can you use to automate certain tasks in your network marketing business?

How can the internet help you reach a wider audience and scale your business?

How can you leverage technology and the internet to create a more efficient and streamlined business process?

What challenges have you faced while incorporating technology into your network marketing business and how have you overcome them?

What are some ways you can continue to stay up-to-date with the latest technology and tools for network marketing?

Have you noticed an increase in success since incorporating technology into your network marketing strategy? Can you share any results or data to support this?

Staying Up-to-Date with the Latest Tools and Strategies for Online Marketing

The world of online marketing is constantly evolving and it's important to stay up-to-date with the latest tools and strategies in order to remain competitive and successful in your network marketing business. The following are some tips for staying informed and up-to-date:

Read Industry Blogs and Websites: Following industry blogs and websites is a great way to stay informed about the latest tools and strategies for online marketing. You can subscribe to blog feeds and newsletters to stay updated with the latest news and trends in the industry.

Attend Conferences and Webinars: Attending conferences and webinars is a great way to learn about the latest tools and strategies for online marketing. You can meet industry experts, network with other network marketers, and learn about the latest trends and technologies in the field.

Join Online Communities: Joining online communities, such as forums and discussion groups, is a great way to stay up-to-date with the latest tools and strategies for online marketing. You can connect with other network marketers and learn from their experiences and best practices.

Conduct Market Research: Conducting market research is a great way to stay informed about the latest trends and technologies in the industry. You can use online tools, such as Google Trends and SEMrush, to track keywords, search terms, and trends related to online marketing.

By following these tips, you can stay informed and up-to-date with the latest tools and strategies for online marketing, and remain competitive and successful in your network marketing business.

Engagement Questions:

What are some of the most important tools and strategies for online marketing in network marketing today?
How do you stay informed and up-to-date with the latest tools and strategies for online marketing?
What are some of the most effective ways to stay up-to-date with the latest trends and technologies in the industry?
How can market research help you stay informed and up-to-date with the latest tools and strategies for online marketing?

Building a Team and Leveraging the Power of Collaboration

One of the key components to success in network marketing is building a strong and supportive team. This can help you leverage the power of collaboration and ensure that everyone is working towards a common goal. A well-functioning team can help you reach new heights, both in terms of revenue and growth. In this chapter, we will discuss how to build a team and how to leverage the power of collaboration to achieve your goals.

The first step in building a team is to identify your target audience and determine what kind of people you want to work with. Consider their skills, interests, and work style when making your decision. It is important to choose people who are aligned with your values and goals and who share a common vision for the future.

Once you have identified your target audience, it is time to start reaching out to them. There are a variety of ways to do this, including networking events, social media, and online groups. Whatever method you choose, be sure to have a clear and compelling message that will attract the right people to your team.

Once you have a team in place, it is important to establish clear roles and responsibilities for each member. This will help to ensure that everyone is on the same page and that everyone knows what is expected of them. You should also consider setting up regular meetings or check-ins to keep everyone in the loop and to ensure that everyone is working towards the same goals.

In addition to building a team, it is also important to leverage the power of collaboration. This can include cross-promoting each other's businesses, working together on projects, and sharing resources and knowledge. By leveraging the power of collaboration, you can help to create a more efficient and effective network marketing business.

Building a team and leveraging the power of collaboration is essential for success in network marketing. By identifying your target audience, reaching out to the right people, and establishing clear roles and responsibilities, you can build a strong and supportive team that will help you achieve your goals.

Engagement Questions:

Who do you want to work with in your network marketing business?
How will you reach out to potential team members?
What are some ways to leverage the power of collaboration in network marketing?

How can you establish clear roles and responsibilities for your team members?

What are some ways to ensure that everyone is working towards the same goals?

CHAPTER 8: SUMMING IT UP - KEY TAKEAWAYS FROM PART 1

Summarizing the key takeaways from the part 1

Encouraging readers to take action and start their journey towards network marketing success

Providing additional resources and support for continued learning and growth.

In this chapter, we will be summarizing the key points covered in Part 1 of the guide to network marketing. This will include a brief overview of the concepts discussed in previous chapters, including understanding your target audience and niche, developing a marketing plan and strategy, finding potential prospects, motivating the spectators, generating leads and prospects online, and utilizing technology and the internet to automate and scale your business.

The purpose of this chapter is to provide a clear and concise summary of the information covered in Part 1, and to encourage readers to take action and start their journey towards network marketing success. By taking the time to review and reflect on the key takeaways from this guide, readers can gain a deeper understanding of the network marketing landscape and develop a solid foundation for their own business.

Additionally, this chapter will provide additional resources and support for continued learning and growth, including recommended books, courses, and online communities. Whether you are just starting out or looking to expand your knowledge, these resources will help you stay up-to-date with the latest tools and strategies for online marketing and network marketing success.

Summarizing the Key Takeaways from Part 1

In Part 1 of this guide, we have covered several key elements to help you build a successful network marketing business. Let's take a moment to summarize the key takeaways from this section:

Understanding the basics of network marketing: We discussed what network marketing is, how it works, and what are the key characteristics of a successful network marketer.

Defining your niche and target audience: We explored how to identify your target audience and what makes them unique, how to find your niche and how to focus on serving their needs and wants.

Developing a marketing plan and strategy: We talked about how to create a marketing plan that is tailored to your business and your target audience. We covered various marketing techniques such as social media campaigns, email marketing, affiliate marketing, and MLM.

Finding potential prospects: We went over the importance of identifying your ideal customer and building a prospect list. We also explored various methods to find potential prospects, both online and offline, and how to nurture your leads.

Motivating the spectators: We discussed how to build relationships with prospects and customers, how to provide value and create trust, and how to overcome objections and close sales.

Generating leads and prospects online: We talked about the importance of online marketing in network marketing, and how to use social media and other online platforms to reach your target audience and build an online presence.

Utilizing technology and the internet: We went over the role of technology and the internet in network marketing, and how to utilize it to automate and scale your business. We also discussed how to stay up-to-date with the latest tools and strategies for online marketing.

These are the key takeaways from Part 1 of this guide. In Part 2, we will explore more advanced techniques and strategies to help you take your network marketing business to the next level. Remember, success in network marketing is not about selling more products or signing up more people, it's about building relationships and serving others. By implementing the concepts covered in Part 1, you will be well on your way to building a successful network marketing business.

Encouraging Readers to Take Action

Congratulations! You have made it through Part 1 of your journey towards network marketing success. Now is the time to put your knowledge into action. You have learned the basics of network marketing, including how to understand your target audience and niche, develop a marketing plan and strategy, identify your ideal customer, motivate prospects, generate leads and prospects online, and utilize technology and the internet to automate and scale your business. It is now time to put these concepts into practice and start building your network marketing empire.

Taking action is the most important step towards success in any venture. While reading and learning about network marketing is important, it is only through taking action that you will begin to see results. To get started, choose one or two concepts from Part 1 that you feel you need to work on the most, and make a plan to implement them. Once you have successfully executed these concepts, move on to the next ones. By breaking down your goals into smaller, manageable steps, you will make the journey much easier and more achievable.

It is important to remember that success in network marketing does not happen overnight. It takes time, effort, and persistence. But, with the right mindset, strategies, and support, anyone can achieve success in network marketing. So, don't be afraid to take the first step towards your network marketing journey. Embrace the learning process, and most importantly, never give up on your goals. With each step you take, you will get closer to realizing your full potential and achieving success in network marketing.

Now is the time to take action. Start building your network marketing empire today!

Additional Resources and Support for Continued Learning and Growth

After going through the first part of this guide, you should have a good understanding of the basics of network marketing and how to get started in this exciting industry. However, there is always more to learn and grow in the world of network marketing, and the key to success is to continuously educate yourself and strive for growth. In this chapter, we will provide you with additional resources and support to help you on your journey towards network marketing success.

Additional Resources

There are countless resources available for network marketers, from online courses and webinars to books and podcasts. Whether you are a seasoned network marketer or just starting out, it's important to seek out new sources of knowledge and inspiration to help you reach your goals. Here are some of the best resources to help you grow your network marketing business:

Books: There are numerous books available on network marketing, including classics like "The Network Marketing Game" by Mary Christensen and "The Ultimate Guide to Network Marketing" by Joe Rubino. These books provide a wealth of information and insights on various aspects of network marketing, including building a team, creating a marketing plan, and overcoming objections.

Online Courses: With the rise of online learning platforms, there are now many courses available for network marketers. These courses offer a more structured learning experience and can be a great way to gain a deeper understanding of specific topics, such as social media marketing or lead generation.

Webinars: Webinars are live online events that allow you to interact with experts in network marketing. These events provide an opportunity to ask questions, network with other network marketers, and learn about the latest strategies and tools for success.

Podcasts: Podcasts are a great way to learn about network marketing on the go. There are many podcasts dedicated to network marketing, and they provide a wealth of information and inspiration to help you grow your business.

Social Media: Social media platforms like Facebook, Instagram, and Twitter are great places to connect with other network marketers, share your experiences, and learn about new strategies and tools.

Support and Community

In addition to resources, it's also important to have support and community to help you on your journey towards network marketing success. Here are some ways to build your network marketing community:

Join a Network Marketing Group: There are many groups on social media and online forums dedicated to network marketing. Joining one of these groups can provide you with a supportive community of network marketers who can offer advice, encouragement, and support.

Attend Network Marketing Events: Network marketing events, such as conferences and workshops, provide an opportunity to meet other network marketers and learn from industry experts. These events can also be a great way to network and build relationships with other network marketers.

Partner with a Mentor: Having a mentor in the network marketing industry can be incredibly helpful in helping you to grow your business. A mentor can provide guidance, advice, and support as you navigate the challenges of network marketing.

In conclusion, network marketing success requires continuous learning, growth, and support. By seeking out additional resources and building a supportive community, you can ensure that you have the tools and support you need to reach your goals and succeed in network marketing.

PART 2
THE BIBLE OF NETWORK MARKETING A-Z

Welcome to Part 2 of The Bible of Network Marketing A-Z, where we dive deeper into the world of network marketing. I appreciate your dedication to starting your home-based business and your eagerness to learn more about this thriving industry. Network marketing is a unique business model that involves the distribution of goods and services from a company to the end consumer through a network of independent distributors.

Every day, people are participating in some form of network marketing, whether they realize it or not. For example, when you try a new restaurant and enjoy it, you're likely to recommend it to your friends, which increases the restaurant's business through word-of-mouth referrals. This is just one example of how we suggest products and services to our friends in our daily lives.

In America, every 11 seconds someone starts a new home-based network marketing business, and 55% of Americans have purchased a network-marketing product or service. However, establishing a successful network marketing business goes beyond just learning what to say and do. Just like any other valuable guidance or self-improvement program, there is no end to the learning process, only a constant journey of growth, knowledge, wisdom, and success.

This volume is designed to provide tools and guidance for both experienced veterans and fresh, beginner distributors in the network marketing industry. The Bible of Network Marketing A-Z will take you on a journey from A to Z, providing a comprehensive understanding of the industry and everything you need to know to succeed in network marketing. Get ready to take your business to the next level!

CHAPTER 9 INTRODUCTION

Definition of Network Marketing
Importance of Network Marketing
Explanation of why people quit in network marketing

Introduction to Network Marketing

Network marketing has become a popular method for individuals to start their own business and achieve financial freedom. It is a multi-level marketing strategy where you can sell products or services and also recruit others to join your business and earn commissions from their sales.

The definition of network marketing is a business model where independent distributors are given the opportunity to earn an income by selling products and services, as well as by sponsoring new members into the business. This creates a network of individuals, who not only sell products but also build their own teams and earn commissions from their efforts.

The importance of network marketing lies in its ability to provide individuals with a flexible and low-cost way to start a business, with the potential for unlimited income. Network marketing allows for the distribution of products and services to reach a wider audience through word-of-mouth referrals and personal relationships, creating a unique and personal marketing experience.

Despite its potential benefits, many individuals still fail in network marketing, leading them to quit within a short period of time. This chapter will explore why people often quit in network marketing and how to overcome those obstacles to achieve success in this business model.

Definition of Network Marketing

Network marketing, also known as multi-level marketing (MLM), is a business model that involves the distribution of goods and services through a network of independent distributors. The main goal of network marketing is to generate revenue through the sales of products and services, as well as through the recruitment of new distributors who are also encouraged to sell the products and services.

The key to network marketing is the creation of a network of distributors who work together to promote and sell the products and services. These distributors earn a commission on their sales, as well as a percentage of the sales generated by their downline, or the distributors they have recruited.

Network marketing is a direct selling method, meaning that the products and services are sold directly to the consumer, rather than through retail stores or other traditional channels. This direct-to-consumer approach helps companies reduce marketing and distribution costs, and also allows distributors to earn a greater percentage of the sales revenue.

In network marketing, the company is responsible for providing training and support to the distributors, and for developing and marketing the products and services. The distributors are responsible for selling the products and services, as well as for recruiting and training new distributors.

Overall, network marketing is a unique business model that offers entrepreneurs the opportunity to build a successful business through sales and recruitment efforts. Whether you are just starting out or are an experienced network marketer, understanding the definition of network marketing is essential to success in this industry.

Importance of Network Marketing

Network marketing has become a popular business model for entrepreneurs, small business owners, and individuals looking for a flexible and low-cost way to start their own business. In today's fast-paced and highly competitive world, it is more important than ever for businesses to find new and innovative ways to reach their target market and achieve their goals. Network marketing provides a unique opportunity for individuals to build their own business and achieve financial independence, while also helping others to do the same.

One of the most important benefits of network marketing is that it offers a low-risk and low-cost alternative to traditional business models. Unlike traditional businesses, which often require significant startup costs and investments in physical assets, network marketing allows individuals to start their own business with minimal upfront costs. This makes it an ideal option for those who want to start their own business but may not have the financial resources to do so.

Another key benefit of network marketing is that it offers a high degree of flexibility. Unlike traditional business models, network marketing allows individuals to work from anywhere, at any time. This allows individuals to balance their work and personal life in a way that suits their unique needs and preferences. Whether you are looking to supplement your income or build a full-time business, network marketing provides a flexible and flexible alternative to traditional business models.

Finally, network marketing provides a unique opportunity for individuals to help others achieve their goals. Whether you are helping others build their own business or simply sharing products and services that you believe in, network marketing allows you to make a positive impact on the lives of others while also building your own success. This creates a sense of fulfillment and satisfaction that is often missing from traditional business models.

In conclusion, network marketing is an important business model that offers a low-risk, low-cost, and flexible alternative to traditional business models. Whether you are looking to supplement your income, start your own business, or make a positive impact on the lives of others, network marketing provides a unique opportunity for individuals to achieve their goals and live their best life.

Explanation of Why People Quit in Network Marketing

Network marketing is an industry that offers an incredible opportunity for anyone who wants to build a successful business from the comfort of their own home. However, despite the opportunities that it presents, a high percentage of people who start a network marketing business quit within the first few months. Understanding why this happens is critical if you want to avoid falling into the same trap and quitting your network marketing journey before you reach your goals.

One of the primary reasons why people quit network marketing is because of the lack of support and guidance from their upline. Many people who start a network marketing business are not experienced business owners, and they require guidance and support from their upline to help them achieve success. Without the proper guidance, many people feel lost and unsure of what to do, and they eventually give up and quit.

Another reason why people quit network marketing is because of the lack of financial results. Many people who start a network marketing business do so with the hope of making a significant income, and when they don't see results right away, they become discouraged and quit. This is often because they are not properly trained on how to market and promote their business, and they don't know how to generate leads and sales.

Finally, people also quit network marketing because they lose motivation and enthusiasm. Building a successful network marketing business takes time, hard work, and dedication, and many people simply don't have what it takes to stay motivated and committed over the long term. When this happens, they quit and look for a more straightforward or easier way to make money.

In conclusion, if you want to succeed in network marketing, it's crucial to understand why people quit and to take steps to avoid falling into the same trap. This means seeking out training and guidance, setting achievable goals, and staying motivated and committed to your business, even when the going gets tough.

CHAPTER 10: A-Z GUIDE TO NETWORK MARKETING SUCCESS

In this chapter, we will explore 26 essential tips for success in network marketing, each represented by a different letter of the alphabet. From "A" for attitude to "Z" for zeal, this comprehensive guide will cover all the key elements you need to master in order to build a successful network marketing business. Whether you are a seasoned veteran or just starting out, this A-Z guide will provide you with actionable insights and practical advice for maximizing your results and achieving your goals in network marketing. Get ready to dive into the world of network marketing and unlock your full potential for success!

A) Automate Processes: Utilizing Technology to Save Time

In today's fast-paced business world, it's essential to make the most of the time you have available. One way to do this is by automating repetitive tasks so that you can focus on more important tasks that require your attention. Network marketing is no different and can benefit greatly from automation. By automating processes, you can free up valuable time that can be spent on other tasks that can help you grow your business.

One of the most common tasks in network marketing is prospecting and following up with leads. This can take a lot of time and energy, and it's easy to miss opportunities if you don't have a system in place to help you stay organized. Fortunately, there are many tools available that can help you automate this process and ensure that you are following up with leads in a timely manner.

Another area where automation can be helpful is in tracking your sales and commissions. By automating this process, you can ensure that you are getting paid for all of your hard work. This can help you stay motivated and focused on growing your business.

Another advantage of automating processes is that it can help you scale your business. By freeing up time and energy, you can focus on building your team and expanding your reach. This can lead to increased sales and commissions, which can help you reach your financial goals more quickly.

Automating processes in network marketing can have a significant impact on your success. By freeing up time and energy, you can focus on the tasks that will help you grow your business and reach your goals. Whether you are a seasoned veteran or a newcomer to network marketing, incorporating technology into your business can help you achieve success.

Engagement Questions

How have you been managing repetitive tasks in your network marketing business so far?

Have you explored the option of automating any processes in your business?

What kind of technology do you currently use to manage your network marketing business?

How do you see automating processes improving the efficiency and productivity of your business?

What specific tasks do you think could be automated to save time in your business?

Have you encountered any challenges when it comes to implementing automation in your business?

How have other successful network marketers used technology to automate their processes?

What resources would you recommend for those looking to learn more about automating processes in network marketing?

In your opinion, how will automation impact the future of network marketing?

How do you plan on utilizing technology to automate processes and save time in your business moving forward?

B) Build relationships: Focus on building strong relationships with prospects and customers.

Building relationships is at the core of network marketing success. The more personal connections you make with your prospects and customers, the more likely they are to trust you, buy from you, and recommend you to others. In this chapter, we will explore how to build strong relationships with your network marketing prospects and customers.

One of the most important things you can do to build relationships is to listen to your prospects and customers. Take the time to get to know them, understand their needs and wants, and find out what they're looking for in a network marketing opportunity. This information will help you to tailor your approach and messaging to meet their specific needs and wants.

Another key element of building relationships is to be authentic and genuine. Don't try to be someone you're not or pretend to have all the answers. Instead, be transparent, honest, and vulnerable. Share your own experiences, successes, and challenges. This will help your prospects and customers to feel more connected to you and to trust you more.

In addition to listening and being authentic, it's also important to be consistent. This means showing up for your prospects and customers on a regular basis, following up with them regularly, and being there for them when they need you. Building strong relationships takes time and effort, but the rewards are well worth it. When you have a solid network of supportive and engaged prospects and customers, your network marketing business will thrive.

Engagement Questions:

What do you think is the most important factor in building relationships with prospects and customers in network marketing?

How do you ensure that you are being authentic and genuine in your interactions with prospects and customers?

How do you keep track of your relationships with prospects and customers and ensure that you are staying in touch with them regularly?

Have you attended any networking events or conferences that have helped you to build relationships in your network marketing business? If so, which ones?

How do you balance the need to build relationships with the need to focus on other aspects of your network marketing business, such as product promotion and sales?

C) Create Valuable Content

Creating valuable content is a crucial aspect of any successful network marketing strategy. By offering helpful information and insights through blog posts, videos, and other forms of content, you can establish yourself as a thought leader in your industry and build trust with your prospects and customers.

There are many different ways to create valuable content, but the key is to focus on providing information that is relevant, useful, and of interest to your target audience. This might include tips and advice on how to use your products or services, information on industry trends and developments, or in-depth guides on specific topics related to your business.

One effective way to create valuable content is to start a blog and post regular articles on a variety of topics related to your business. This can help you to reach a wider audience, engage with your followers, and build your brand. Additionally, you can use social media platforms, such as Facebook and Twitter, to share your blog posts and reach even more people.

Another way to create valuable content is to produce videos that showcase your products or services, or provide educational information on a particular topic. These can be posted on your website, YouTube channel, or other video hosting platforms, and shared on social media to help increase your visibility and reach.

Regardless of the type of content you choose to create, the key is to be consistent, engaging, and always focused on providing value to your audience. By doing this, you can establish yourself as an authority in your industry, and build strong relationships with your prospects and customers.

Engagement Questions:

What types of content have you found to be most valuable to your target audience?

How do you ensure that the content you create is relevant and of interest to your prospects and customers?

What strategies have you used to promote your content and increase its reach?

How do you measure the success of your content marketing efforts?

What tips do you have for creating engaging and impactful videos for your network marketing business?

D) Develop a strong brand: Define your brand and communicate it consistently through all marketing materials.

When it comes to network marketing, having a strong brand can be the key to success. A strong brand helps you stand out from your competitors and communicate your value proposition to your prospects and customers. It's a crucial aspect of building a successful network marketing business.

A brand is much more than just a logo or a tagline. It encompasses everything about your business, from the products or services you offer, to the way you communicate with your target audience. It's a representation of your company's unique value proposition, personality, and culture.

The first step in developing a strong brand is to define your brand. This involves figuring out what makes your business unique and what sets you apart from your competitors. It's important to understand your target audience and what they are looking for in a network marketing opportunity. Once you have a clear understanding of your target audience and what sets your business apart, you can start to build your brand around these key elements.

Once you have a clear definition of your brand, it's time to communicate it consistently through all your marketing materials. This includes your website, business cards, social media accounts, and any other marketing materials you use to reach your target audience. Consistency is key when it comes to building a strong brand, as it helps build trust and recognition with your audience.

It's also important to invest in professional design for your marketing materials. A well-designed logo and website can go a long way in helping you establish your brand and create a professional image.

In conclusion, developing a strong brand is essential for building a successful network marketing business. By defining your brand, communicating it consistently, and investing in professional design, you can create a strong and recognizable brand that sets you apart from your competitors and helps you build a thriving network marketing business.

Engagement Questions

How would you define your personal brand?
How does your brand reflect your values and unique qualities?

What makes your brand different from your competitors?

How do you ensure your brand stays consistent across all your marketing materials?

What steps have you taken to strengthen your brand image and messaging?

In what ways can you effectively communicate your brand to your target audience?

How has having a strong brand impacted your business success?

How do you continuously evaluate and evolve your brand to stay relevant?

What resources or tools have you found helpful in developing and promoting your brand?

How do you stay inspired and motivated to maintain and improve your brand image?

E) Engage with your audience: Respond to comments and questions from your audience to keep them engaged.

Networking marketing is all about building strong relationships and connecting with your audience. In order to keep your audience engaged, it is essential to be responsive to their comments and questions. This not only shows that you value their input, but also helps to build trust and credibility with your audience.

One of the best ways to engage with your audience is by regularly responding to comments and questions on your social media platforms, blogs, and other forms of content. This could include responding to comments on your Facebook page, answering questions in a LinkedIn group, or replying to direct messages on Instagram.

Another effective way to engage with your audience is by hosting live events or webinars. This allows you to interact with your audience in real-time and answer any questions they may have.

When engaging with your audience, it is important to be personal and authentic. People want to feel like they are connecting with a real person, not just a brand. Make sure to use your own voice and share your own experiences and insights.

It is also important to be consistent with your engagement. Regularly responding to comments and questions shows that you are committed to building a strong relationship with your audience.

Finally, be sure to track your engagement metrics and measure the success of your efforts. This will help you to continuously improve your engagement strategies and better understand what is resonating with your audience.

Engagement Questions

How often do you respond to comments and questions from your audience?

How do you keep your audience engaged with your brand?

What tools do you use to track engagement metrics and measure the success of your engagement efforts?

How do you ensure that your engagement with your audience is personal and authentic?

How do you stay consistent with your engagement efforts?

F) Follow up with leads: Consistently follow up with leads to build trust and convert them into customers.

Following up with leads is an essential aspect of successful network marketing. It is a process of building trust and nurturing relationships with prospects who have shown an interest in your products or services. In order to convert these prospects into customers, it is important to follow up with them consistently and provide them with valuable information about your offerings.

Why is following up with leads important?

Leads are potential customers who have expressed an interest in your products or services, but they may not be ready to make a purchase yet. By following up with leads, you can help build trust and establish a relationship with them. This can help increase the likelihood of converting them into customers and growing your business.

How to effectively follow up with leads?

Personalize your approach: Customize your follow-up message based on the lead's specific interests and needs.

Provide value: Offer valuable information and insights that can help the lead make an informed decision.

Be consistent: Follow up with leads at regular intervals to keep the conversation going and maintain their interest.

Listen to their needs: Pay attention to what the lead is saying and respond accordingly.

Use technology: Utilize automation tools to streamline your follow-up process and ensure that leads receive consistent, timely communications.

By following these tips, you can effectively follow up with leads and increase your chances of converting them into customers. In network marketing, building strong relationships with prospects and customers is key to success, and consistent follow-up is a critical component of that process.

G) Generate leads: Use online platforms and tools to generate leads for your business.

Lead generation is the process of attracting and converting prospects into customers. In network marketing, lead generation is crucial to the success of your business. The more leads you generate, the more potential customers you have to sell your products or services to. The goal of lead generation is to get as many people as possible interested in your business and what you have to offer.

There are several ways to generate leads in network marketing, but one of the most effective ways is through the use of online platforms and tools. The internet provides a wealth of opportunities to reach a large audience, and there are a number of tools and platforms that can help you to generate leads more effectively.

One of the most important things to consider when generating leads online is your website. Your website should be optimized for search engines and designed to provide value to your visitors. It should be easy to navigate, visually appealing, and have a clear call-to-action. A well-designed website can help you to generate leads, build your brand, and provide valuable information to your audience.

Another way to generate leads is through social media. Social media platforms like Facebook, Instagram, and Twitter provide a massive audience that you can reach out to. By creating valuable content and engaging with your audience, you can attract new leads and build relationships with them. You can also use social media advertising to target specific demographics and reach a larger audience.

Email marketing is another powerful tool that can help you to generate leads. By sending out regular emails to your subscribers, you can keep them engaged and interested in your business. You can use email marketing to promote your products or services, share valuable information, and build relationships with your subscribers.

In conclusion, generating leads is an important part of network marketing, and by utilizing online platforms and tools, you can reach a larger audience, build your brand, and grow your business.

H) Host events: Host events to bring prospects and customers together and build relationships.

Hosting events can be a powerful way to build relationships with prospects and customers. In the world of network marketing, events can be used to educate, inspire, and connect people. By providing a platform for like-minded individuals to gather and exchange ideas, you can build a strong and engaged community around your brand.

There are a variety of events you can host, including workshops, product demonstrations, training sessions, and networking events. Each of these types of events can serve a different purpose, but they all have the potential to bring people together and strengthen your relationships with prospects and customers.

When hosting events, it's important to create a welcoming and inclusive atmosphere. Encourage attendees to engage with one another and participate in activities or discussions. You can also incorporate games or challenges to encourage attendees to get to know each other and build relationships.

One of the key benefits of hosting events is that they can help you build trust with your audience. By providing valuable information and insights, and by creating a space for people to connect and engage, you can establish yourself as an expert in your field and build strong relationships with prospects and customers.

In addition to building relationships, hosting events can also help you generate leads for your business. By providing an opportunity for people to learn about your products and services, you can generate interest and encourage prospects to take action.

When hosting events, it's important to have a clear goal in mind. Whether you're looking to build relationships, generate leads, or educate your audience, having a clear goal will help you to focus your efforts and maximize the impact of your event.

By hosting events and bringing prospects and customers together, you can create a powerful platform for building relationships, generating leads, and growing your network marketing business. So don't be afraid to get creative and think outside the box when it comes to hosting events for your business.

Engagement Questions

What kind of events have you hosted in the past to promote your business?

How do you choose the right type of event to host for your target audience?

How do you measure the success of your events?

What are some unique ways you have used events to build relationships with prospects and customers?

What are some tips for making your events stand out and be memorable for attendees?

How do you follow up with attendees after the event to continue the relationship building process?

Have you ever faced any challenges when hosting events? If so, how did you overcome them?

How do you use events to promote your brand and generate leads for your business?

What role do events play in your overall marketing strategy?

How do you balance the cost of hosting events with the potential benefits they bring to your business?

I) Implement a system: Create a systematic approach to your marketing to ensure consistency and efficiency.

One of the keys to success in network marketing is having a systematic approach to your marketing efforts. This involves creating a step-by-step process for every aspect of your marketing, from generating leads to following up with customers. By implementing a system, you can ensure consistency in your marketing efforts and maximize your results.

A well-designed marketing system can help you streamline your processes, eliminate inefficiencies, and increase productivity. This, in turn, can help you save time and increase your profitability. The key is to find a system that works for you and your business and to stick with it over time.

When implementing a marketing system, there are several important steps to keep in mind. First, you need to define your target audience and understand their needs and preferences. This will help you tailor your marketing efforts to their specific needs and increase your chances of success.

Next, you should develop a clear strategy for how you will reach your target audience. This could involve using a variety of online and offline marketing techniques, such as social media, email marketing, and events.

Finally, you should track and measure your results to ensure that your system is working effectively. This can be done through various metrics, such as website traffic, lead generation, and conversion rates. By analyzing this data, you can make adjustments to your system as needed to maximize your results.

In conclusion, implementing a system in your network marketing efforts can help you achieve success and reach your goals. By creating a consistent and efficient approach, you can save time, increase productivity, and ultimately increase your profitability.

Engagement Questions

How do you currently approach your marketing efforts?

What processes do you have in place to ensure consistency and efficiency in your marketing?

How have you streamlined your marketing efforts in the past?

Have you implemented any systems or frameworks to help with your marketing efforts? If so, what were the results?

What do you think would be the biggest benefits of implementing a systematic approach to your marketing?

What challenges do you anticipate in implementing a systematic approach to your marketing?

How do you plan to overcome these challenges?

How will you measure the success of your systematic approach to marketing?

Have you seen other businesses successfully implement a systematic approach to their marketing? If so, what were some key elements of their approach?

How do you plan to continually improve and evolve your marketing system over time?

J) Join online communities: Participate in online communities relevant to your niche to build relationships and generate leads.

One of the key components of successful network marketing is having the ability to track your progress and make data-driven decisions. This requires you to have a clear understanding of what you want to achieve and how you will measure your progress towards your goals. In this chapter, we will discuss the importance of keeping track of your progress and the tools and metrics you can use to do so.

Keeping track of your progress is essential for a number of reasons. First, it allows you to see what is working and what is not. This information can then be used to make adjustments to your strategy and approach in order to achieve better results. Additionally, tracking your progress helps you to stay focused and motivated. When you can see that you are making progress towards your goals, it can help to keep you motivated and focused on what you need to do next.

There are a number of tools and metrics that you can use to track your progress. Some of the most common include web analytics tools, social media analytics, email marketing analytics, and customer relationship management (CRM) software. These tools provide valuable insights into your audience, the impact of your marketing efforts, and the effectiveness of your sales and marketing activities.

When choosing the right tools and metrics to track your progress, it is important to consider your goals and the type of data you want to collect. For example, if you are trying to generate leads, you may want to focus on tracking the number of website visitors and leads generated through your website. If you are trying to increase sales, you may want to focus on tracking conversion rates, customer lifetime value, and customer acquisition cost.

In conclusion, keeping track of your progress is a crucial aspect of successful network marketing. By using the right tools and metrics, you can make data-driven decisions, stay focused and motivated, and measure the impact of your efforts. By doing so, you can continuously improve and achieve your goals in network marketing.

K) Keep track of your progress: Use tools and metrics to track your progress and make data-driven decisions.

One of the key components of successful network marketing is having the ability to track your progress and make data-driven decisions. This requires you to have a clear understanding of what you want to achieve and how you will measure your progress towards your goals. In this chapter, we will discuss the importance of keeping track of your progress and the tools and metrics you can use to do so.

Keeping track of your progress is essential for a number of reasons. First, it allows you to see what is working and what is not. This information can then be used to make adjustments to your strategy and approach in order to achieve better results. Additionally, tracking your progress helps you to stay focused and motivated. When you can see that you are making progress towards your goals, it can help to keep you motivated and focused on what you need to do next.

There are a number of tools and metrics that you can use to track your progress. Some of the most common include web analytics tools, social media analytics, email marketing analytics, and customer relationship management (CRM) software. These tools provide valuable insights into your audience, the impact of your marketing efforts, and the effectiveness of your sales and marketing activities.

When choosing the right tools and metrics to track your progress, it is important to consider your goals and the type of data you want to collect. For example, if you are trying to generate leads, you may want to focus on tracking the number of website visitors and leads generated through your website. If you are trying to increase sales, you may want to focus on tracking conversion rates, customer lifetime value, and customer acquisition cost.

In conclusion, keeping track of your progress is a crucial aspect of successful network marketing. By using the right tools and metrics, you can make data-driven decisions, stay focused and motivated, and measure the impact of your efforts. By doing so, you can continuously improve and achieve your goals in network marketing.

Engagement Questions

What metrics do you use to track your marketing progress?
How do you ensure consistency in your tracking process?

How do you use data to make informed decisions about your marketing strategy?

Have you noticed any patterns or trends in your marketing progress that have helped guide your decisions?

How do you stay on top of new technologies and tools that can help you better track your progress?

How do you communicate your progress to your team and stakeholders?

How do you use data to identify areas for improvement in your marketing efforts?

What steps have you taken to ensure your tracking process is as accurate and effective as possible?

How do you prioritize which metrics to track and why?

How have your tracking efforts impacted the overall success of your marketing initiatives?

L) Leverage the power of partnerships: Collaborate with other businesses and individuals to reach new audiences and increase your impact.

Collaborating with other businesses and individuals can have a powerful impact on your network marketing efforts. By partnering with others, you can reach new audiences, increase your exposure, and potentially gain new customers. In this chapter, we will discuss the benefits of leveraging partnerships and how to do it effectively.

Partnerships can take many forms, including joint ventures, affiliate marketing, co-marketing campaigns, and more. Whatever form your partnership takes, the key to success is building strong relationships with your partners. When you work closely with others who share your goals and values, you can achieve great things together.

To effectively leverage the power of partnerships, you must first identify potential partners who align with your brand and target audience. Look for businesses and individuals who complement your offerings and can help you reach new audiences. You should also consider their reputation and the value they can bring to the partnership.

Once you have identified potential partners, it's time to start building relationships. This can involve reaching out to them through social media, attending events, or engaging in other forms of communication. As you build relationships, be sure to communicate openly and clearly about your goals, expectations, and any specific requirements.

Once you have established partnerships, it's important to keep the momentum going. This means staying in touch with your partners, keeping them informed about your progress, and finding ways to continuously build and grow your partnership.

In summary, leveraging the power of partnerships can have a significant impact on your network marketing efforts. By working closely with other businesses and individuals, you can reach new audiences, increase your exposure, and potentially gain new customers.

Engagement Questions:

What benefits have you seen from collaborating with other businesses and individuals?

How do you identify potential partners for your network marketing efforts?

What steps do you take to build strong relationships with your partners?

How do you ensure that your partnerships remain productive and effective over time?

M) Measure your results: Regularly measure your results to track your progress and make data-driven decisions.

One of the key elements to a successful network marketing strategy is the ability to measure and track your results. This involves regularly evaluating the effectiveness of your marketing efforts and using data to make informed decisions about how to improve. Measuring your results helps you determine what is working well, what needs improvement, and where to allocate your resources for maximum impact.

There are a variety of tools and metrics you can use to measure your results. Some of the most common metrics used in network marketing include conversion rates, customer lifetime value, return on investment, and customer satisfaction. By tracking these metrics over time, you can see how your marketing efforts are impacting your business and make data-driven decisions to optimize your strategies.

In addition to using metrics to measure your results, it's also important to regularly review and evaluate your strategies and processes. This may involve conducting surveys or focus groups with your customers, analyzing customer feedback, or talking to your team members about what they're seeing in the field.

By taking a systematic approach to measuring and tracking your results, you can ensure that your network marketing efforts are continuously improving and that you're making the most of your resources. This will help you achieve your goals and build a successful, sustainable business.

Engagement Questions

How do you currently measure your marketing results?

What metrics do you consider most important in tracking the success of your marketing efforts?

How often do you measure your results, and what tools do you use to do so?

What challenges have you faced in accurately measuring your results, and how have you overcome them?

Have you ever made significant changes to your marketing strategy based on your results data? Can you share an example?

In your opinion, what is the most important benefit of regularly measuring your marketing results?

How do you ensure that your team is consistently tracking and using the data gathered from measuring results?

How has regularly measuring your results impacted your overall marketing strategy and success?

What advice would you give to others who are just starting to track their marketing results?

How do you plan on continuing to improve your measurement and analysis processes in the future?

N) Network with influencers: Connect with influencers in your niche to leverage their audience and reach new prospects.

Networking with influencers can be a valuable strategy for growing your network marketing business. By connecting with individuals who have a large following in your niche, you can tap into their audience and reach new prospects. In this chapter, we'll explore the benefits of network with influencers and the steps you can take to make the most of this strategy.

Networking with influencers can help you:

Reach a wider audience: Influencers have a built-in audience that trusts them and is likely to be interested in what they have to offer. By connecting with influencers, you can tap into this audience and reach new prospects who might not have heard of your business otherwise.

Establish credibility: Working with influencers can help you establish credibility and build your reputation in your niche. Influencers are seen as experts in their field, and by partnering with them, you can demonstrate your expertise and build trust with your audience.

Drive traffic to your website: Influencers can drive traffic to your website and help you increase your visibility online. They can share your content with their audience, which can help you reach new prospects and grow your business.

To network with influencers, you can start by:

Identifying influencers in your niche: Look for individuals who have a large following in your target market and who are active on social media and other online platforms.

Building a relationship: Reach out to the influencer and start building a relationship with them. Offer to share their content, leave comments on their posts, and engage with them on social media.

Collaborating: Once you've established a relationship, you can look for opportunities to collaborate with the influencer. This could include hosting a joint webinar, offering a joint product, or working on a joint marketing campaign.

By networking with influencers, you can tap into their audience and reach new prospects, establish credibility, and grow your business.

Engagement Questions

How have you leveraged influencer partnerships in your own marketing efforts?

What strategies have you found most effective for building relationships with influencers?

How do you identify the right influencers for your brand and niche?

What metrics do you use to measure the success of your influencer marketing campaigns?

How do you balance the need for authenticity with the potential commercial benefits of partnering with influencers?

How do you handle any conflicts or differences that may arise during an influencer partnership?

In your experience, what are the key factors that determine the success of an influencer partnership?

How do you ensure that your brand's messaging is aligned with the influencer's values and brand image?

How do you stay on top of changes in the influencer marketing landscape and adapt your strategy accordingly?

What advice do you have for businesses just starting to explore influencer marketing?

O) Optimize your website: Ensure your website is optimized for search engines and mobile devices to improve visibility and engagement.

A well-optimized website is essential for any successful network marketing campaign. In today's digital age, a large portion of your target audience will find your business through online searches and your website will be their first impression. By optimizing your website, you can improve visibility, engagement, and conversion rates.

To optimize your website, start by ensuring that it is easy to navigate and has a clean, professional design. Make sure that your website is mobile-friendly, as more and more people are accessing the internet on their mobile devices. Also, consider the user experience and focus on providing a positive experience for your website visitors.

Another important aspect of website optimization is search engine optimization (SEO). SEO involves using keywords, meta descriptions, and other techniques to improve your website's ranking in search engine results pages (SERPs). This can help you reach more people and drive more traffic to your website.

In conclusion, optimizing your website is crucial for the success of your network marketing campaign. By improving your website's visibility, engagement, and user experience, you can reach more prospects and grow your business.

Engagement Questions:

What are the key elements of a well-optimized website?
How can you improve the user experience on your website?
Why is it important to make your website mobile-friendly?
Can you explain the basics of search engine optimization (SEO)?
How does website optimization impact your network marketing efforts?

P) Personalize your marketing: Personalize your marketing to build strong relationships with prospects and customers.

Personalization is key in building strong relationships with prospects and customers. The more you understand and cater to their individual needs and preferences, the more likely they are to engage with your business and become loyal customers. Personalizing your marketing can also help to differentiate you from your competition, making you stand out and leaving a lasting impression.

Personalizing your marketing can be done in a variety of ways, from customizing emails and communication to offering personalized recommendations and promotions. You can also use technology, such as customer relationship management (CRM) software, to gather and analyze data on your prospects and customers, and use this information to create targeted marketing campaigns.

By taking the time to personalize your marketing, you are not only showing your prospects and customers that you value them, but also increasing the likelihood of building long-lasting relationships that drive business growth and success.

Engagement Questions

How do you currently personalize your marketing efforts for your prospects and customers?

Can you share an example of a successful personalized marketing campaign you have implemented?

How do you collect and utilize customer data to personalize your marketing efforts?

What benefits have you seen from personalizing your marketing efforts?

How do you balance personalization with privacy concerns for your customers?

In what ways do you think personalization will impact the future of marketing?

How do you measure the success of personalized marketing campaigns?

What steps can be taken to improve the personalization of marketing efforts for a business?

How do you stay creative and innovative in your approach to personalizing marketing?

What role do customer feedback and engagement play in personalizing marketing efforts?

Q) Qualify your leads: Use a lead qualification process to identify the most promising prospects for your business.

Network marketing is all about building relationships with prospects and converting them into customers. To do this effectively, it's important to focus your efforts on the prospects who are most likely to buy from you. This is where lead qualification comes in. Lead qualification is the process of identifying the prospects who are most likely to be interested in your products or services. By qualifying your leads, you can prioritize your efforts and focus your time and resources on the prospects who are most likely to convert.

The lead qualification process typically involves gathering information about your prospects, such as their needs, interests, and budget. You can use this information to determine which prospects are most likely to be a good fit for your business. There are a number of different lead qualification metrics that you can use, including the BANT (Budget, Authority, Need, and Timeline) method.

By using a lead qualification process, you can improve your conversion rates and increase the efficiency of your marketing efforts. This can lead to better results and a higher return on investment for your business.

Engagement Questions

What are the benefits of lead qualification in network marketing?

How can you gather information about your prospects to help qualify them?

What are some common lead qualification metrics and methods?

How can you use lead qualification to prioritize your marketing efforts and improve your conversion rates?

Can you think of an example of a time when you qualified a lead and it resulted in a successful conversion?

What are some common mistakes to avoid when qualifying leads in network marketing?

R) Reach out to your audience: Use email, social media, and other platforms to reach out to your audience and build relationships.

In the world of marketing, one of the most important tasks is reaching out to your audience and building relationships with them. There are many different ways to do this, from traditional methods like email and direct mail to newer platforms like social media. No matter which channels you choose to use, the key to success is being intentional and strategic about how you engage with your audience.

Reaching out to your audience means more than just sending out promotional messages. It means taking the time to listen to their needs and interests, responding to their questions and concerns, and providing valuable information and insights that will help them solve their problems. When done right, this type of engagement can help you build trust and credibility with your audience, which will make it much easier to turn them into customers.

In this chapter, we'll explore some of the best strategies and tools for reaching out to your audience and building relationships through communication. Whether you're just starting out or you've been in the marketing game for years, these tips will help you make the most of your efforts and achieve your goals.

Identify your target audience: Before you can effectively reach out to your audience, you need to know who they are and what they care about. This will help you create messages that are relevant, engaging, and appealing.

Choose the right channels: There are many different channels you can use to reach out to your audience, including email, social media, direct mail, and more. Consider which channels will work best for your target audience and your business.

Create compelling content: Whether you're sending an email, posting on social media, or writing a blog post, it's important to create content that is interesting, informative, and valuable to your audience.

Measure your results: Regularly measure your results to see what's working and what's not. Use tools like Google Analytics, social media analytics, and email marketing analytics to track your progress and make data-driven decisions.

Engage with your audience: Respond to comments and questions from your audience, and encourage them to share their thoughts and ideas with you. This will help you build stronger relationships and foster a sense of community.

Reaching out to your audience is a critical part of any successful marketing strategy. By using the right channels, creating compelling content, and engaging with your audience, you'll be able to build strong relationships and drive real results for your business.

S) Segment your audience: Segment your audience based on demographics, interests, and behaviors to target them more effectively.

As a network marketer, it's important to understand the unique needs and interests of your audience. By segmenting your audience into smaller, more targeted groups, you can create more personalized and effective marketing campaigns. In this chapter, we will explore the key elements of audience segmentation and how to use this information to reach your target audience.

What is audience segmentation?
Audience segmentation is the process of dividing a large group of people into smaller, more manageable groups based on shared characteristics. This can include demographic information such as age, gender, location, and income, as well as interests and behaviors such as purchasing habits, preferences, and attitudes towards your products or services.

Why is audience segmentation important?
Segmenting your audience allows you to tailor your marketing efforts to the specific needs and preferences of each group. This leads to more effective and efficient marketing campaigns, as you can reach your target audience with the most relevant information and messaging. Additionally, segmenting your audience can help you to identify new opportunities for growth and engagement, allowing you to expand your reach and impact.

How to segment your audience

To effectively segment your audience, you need to gather data about their demographics, interests, and behaviors. This information can be obtained through surveys, customer feedback, and market research, as well as through the use of tools and technologies such as web analytics and social media listening.

Once you have this information, you can use it to group your audience into smaller segments based on shared characteristics. For example, you might segment your audience based on age, income, location, or purchasing habits.

Engagement Questions:

How have you segmented your audience in the past? What data did you use and what were the results?

How do you plan to gather data on your target audience's demographics, interests, and behaviors?

How will you use this information to create more personalized and effective marketing campaigns?

What challenges have you faced in audience segmentation and how have you overcome them?

How do you measure the success of your audience segmentation efforts and make adjustments as needed?

T) Test and optimize: Regularly test different aspects of your marketing to optimize for the best results.

As a business owner, it's essential to continually evaluate and improve your marketing strategy to reach your goals and drive success. One way to do this is through testing and optimization, where you make small changes to your marketing and see the impact they have on your results. By regularly testing and optimizing, you can identify what's working well and what needs improvement, and make data-driven decisions to maximize your marketing efforts.

Engagement Questions:

Why is testing and optimization important for your marketing strategy?
How do you set up a testing plan for your marketing?
What types of tests can you run to evaluate different aspects of your marketing?
How do you measure the results of your tests and use the data to make informed decisions about your marketing?
What are some common challenges that businesses face when implementing a testing and optimization plan?
How can you ensure that your tests accurately reflect the impact of your marketing changes?
How can you apply the results of your tests to improve your overall marketing strategy and drive better results?

U) Utilize data: Use data and analytics to inform your marketing strategy and make data-driven decisions.

In today's data-driven world, it's essential to have a deep understanding of your audience, their behaviors, and preferences. By leveraging data and analytics, you can make informed decisions about your marketing strategy and improve your results. In this chapter, we'll discuss how to use data to drive your marketing efforts and achieve your business goals.

Segment your audience:
One of the key steps to utilizing data in your marketing strategy is to segment your audience. This means dividing your target market into smaller groups based on demographics, interests, and behaviors. By doing this, you can tailor your marketing efforts to each group, delivering messages that are relevant and appealing to them.

Analyze your data:

Once you've segmented your audience, you'll want to analyze the data you have on them. This could include website traffic, social media engagement, email open rates, and more. By analyzing this data, you'll gain a deeper understanding of what's working and what's not in your marketing efforts, allowing you to make informed decisions about how to optimize your approach.

Test and optimize:

Regular testing and optimization are crucial to improving the effectiveness of your marketing efforts. Whether you're experimenting with different messaging, calls to action, or marketing channels, it's important to test and measure the results of each change you make. This will help you identify what works best and continually improve your results.

Make data-driven decisions:

By leveraging data in your marketing efforts, you'll be able to make data-driven decisions. This means basing your marketing strategies on real data and insights, rather than assumptions or guesses. With a data-driven approach, you can be confident that your efforts will be well-informed and effective in driving your business forward.

Engagement Questions:

How do you currently use data in your marketing efforts?

What challenges have you faced when trying to segment your audience?

Can you share an example of a successful test you've run in your marketing efforts?

How do you ensure that your marketing decisions are based on data and insights?

What tools or software do you use to analyze your marketing data?

How do you measure the success of your marketing efforts?

What steps do you take to continually improve your marketing strategies based on data and insights?

How do you balance the use of data with creative and innovative marketing ideas?

V) Validate your ideas: Validate your marketing ideas through research and testing before investing significant time and resources.

One of the biggest mistakes that businesses can make is to invest significant time and resources into a marketing strategy without first validating the idea. Without proper validation, there is a risk of wasting valuable resources on a marketing strategy that may not produce the desired results. To avoid this, it is essential to validate your marketing ideas through research and testing before making a significant investment.

To validate your marketing ideas, consider the following steps:

Define your target audience: Who are you trying to reach with your marketing efforts? Understanding your target audience will help you to tailor your marketing efforts to their needs and interests.

Research your market: Conduct market research to understand the needs, wants, and behaviors of your target audience. Use surveys, focus groups, and other research methods to gather valuable insights.

Conduct a competitor analysis: Study your competitors to understand their strengths and weaknesses, and identify opportunities for differentiation.

Test your ideas: Before investing significant time and resources into a marketing strategy, test your ideas on a small scale to determine their effectiveness. Use split testing, A/B testing, or other methods to determine what works best for your business.

Gather feedback: Collect feedback from your target audience and customers to understand their thoughts and opinions on your marketing ideas.

Use this feedback to make improvements and optimize your marketing strategy.

By taking these steps to validate your marketing ideas, you can be confident in your investment and increase your chances of success. Remember that research and testing should be an ongoing process to ensure that your marketing efforts remain effective and relevant.

Engagement Questions:

What steps do you take to validate your marketing ideas before investing significant time and resources?

How do you gather feedback from your target audience to inform your marketing efforts?

What methods do you use to test your marketing ideas and determine their effectiveness?

How do you stay up-to-date with market research and competitor analysis to inform your marketing strategy?

How do you measure the success of your marketing efforts and make data-driven decisions?

W) Work on your brand: Continuously work on your brand to ensure it is communicating the right message and appealing to your target audience.

Having a strong brand is critical for success in any market. Your brand is more than just your logo or tagline, it is the entire experience that your prospects and customers have with your business. A strong brand helps to differentiate you from your competitors and build trust with your target audience. In this chapter, we will discuss why it is important to continuously work on your brand and how to do it effectively.

Why Work on Your Brand?

Establish a strong and recognizable identity
Differentiate yourself from competitors
Create a sense of trust and reliability with your audience
Attract and retain customers
Increase brand recognition and awareness
How to Work on Your Brand

Know your audience: Understanding your target audience is critical to creating a brand that resonates with them. This means researching their demographics, interests, and behaviors to ensure your brand speaks to their needs and preferences.

Define your brand values: Your brand values are the core principles that drive your business and inform your decision-making. Take the time to define these values and ensure they align with the needs of your target audience.

Communicate your brand consistently: Your brand should be communicated consistently across all marketing materials, from your website to your social media presence. This consistency helps to build brand recognition and reinforces your message with your audience.

Continuously evaluate and adjust: Your brand should evolve and change over time as your business grows and your target audience evolves. Continuously evaluate your brand and make adjustments as needed to ensure it continues to resonate with your audience.

By continuously working on your brand, you can ensure that your message resonates with your target audience and that your brand remains strong and recognizable. This, in turn, will help you attract and retain customers and increase your impact in your market.

Engagement Questions:

How well do you know your target audience? What steps can you take to learn more about them?

What are your brand values? How do they align with the needs and preferences of your target audience?

How consistent is your brand across all marketing materials? Are there any areas where you could improve consistency?

How do you continuously evaluate and adjust your brand over time? What metrics do you use to track your progress?

In what ways could you improve the way you communicate your brand to your target audience?

X) experiment with new tactics: Continuously experiment with new marketing tactics to find new ways to reach your target audience.

Marketing is constantly evolving, and new tactics are emerging all the time. To stay ahead of the curve, it's essential to continuously experiment with new ways to reach your target audience. This can help you find new and effective ways to connect with your prospects and customers, and grow your business.

In this chapter, we'll explore the importance of experimenting with new marketing tactics, and offer some tips for how to do it effectively. We'll also discuss some of the challenges you may face when trying new things, and provide strategies for overcoming them.

The key to success with experimenting with new tactics is to approach it with an open mind and a willingness to learn. By trying new things, you can learn what works and what doesn't, and use that knowledge to make your marketing more effective. So let's dive in!

Engagement Questions:

What new marketing tactics have you tried in the past? What were the results?

What are some marketing tactics that you're curious about, but haven't tried yet?

How do you evaluate the success of a new marketing tactic? What metrics do you use?

What challenges have you faced when experimenting with new marketing tactics? How did you overcome them?

What is one marketing tactic that you would like to experiment with in the near future? Why?

How do you balance the need to try new things with the need to stick with what works?

What resources or support do you need to experiment with new marketing tactics?

How do you communicate the results of your experiments with others in your organization?

How do you ensure that you are learning from your experiments, and using that knowledge to improve your marketing?

What advice would you give to someone who is just starting to experiment with new marketing tactics?

Y) Yield great results: Consistently implement and refine your marketing strategy to yield great results.

Marketing is a continuous process that requires consistent implementation and refinement. To yield great results, it's essential to have a solid marketing strategy in place and to continually evaluate and adjust it as needed. In this chapter, you'll learn how to create a results-driven marketing plan that helps you reach your goals and grow your business.

You'll discover the importance of consistent implementation, including how to:

Establish clear marketing goals
Develop a plan of action to reach those goals
Monitor and measure your progress
Make data-driven decisions to optimize your strategy
You'll also learn the value of refinement, including:

Identifying areas of your marketing that need improvement
Experimenting with new tactics
Staying up-to-date on industry trends and technology advancements
By consistently implementing and refining your marketing strategy, you can yield great results for your business. This chapter will provide you with the tools and knowledge you need to make it happen.

2) Zero in on your target audience: Focus your marketing efforts on reaching your target audience to maximize impact and results.

In today's fast-paced business world, it's more important than ever to make the most of your marketing efforts. With so many channels and options available, it can be difficult to know where to start. However, the key to success is to focus your efforts on reaching your target audience. By zeroing in on your target audience, you can maximize the impact and results of your marketing efforts.

In this chapter, we will explore the importance of focusing on your target audience and how to do it effectively. We will cover the following topics:

Understanding your target audience: Define your target audience by considering their demographics, interests, behaviors, and pain points.

Identifying your target audience's needs: Research your target audience to gain insights into their needs and preferences.

Focusing your marketing efforts: Use the information you have gathered to create a targeted marketing strategy that reaches your target audience where they are.

Measuring success: Use tools and metrics to track your progress and make data-driven decisions.

CHAPTER 11
UNDERSTANDING THE BASICS OF
NETWORK MARKETING

What is Network Marketing
The Benefits of Network Marketing
The Potential Earnings in Network Marketing

Network marketing, also known as multi-level marketing, is a direct selling strategy that involves promoting and selling products through a network of independent contractors or distributors. This business model has become increasingly popular over the years, attracting entrepreneurs and individuals looking for an alternative to traditional employment.

In this chapter, we will dive into the basics of network marketing and explore what it is, the benefits of participating in this business model, and the potential earnings one can achieve. Whether you are new to network marketing or looking to expand your knowledge, this chapter will provide a comprehensive overview of this exciting and dynamic industry.

From the benefits of being your own boss to the potential for unlimited income, network marketing offers a unique opportunity for individuals to build their own business and achieve financial independence. With a clear understanding of the basics, you will be well on your way to success in the world of network marketing.

What is Network Marketing

Network marketing is a type of direct selling business model that has been gaining popularity over the years. In this model, individuals act as independent business owners and sell products or services through a network of their own personal contacts. This chapter will explore what network marketing is, its benefits, and the potential earnings that can be achieved through this business model.

Network marketing is a business model in which products or services are marketed and sold through a network of independent business owners, also known as network marketers or distributors. These individuals are incentivized to build their own network of customers and recruit other business owners to join their team, creating a chain of distribution. The sales made by each individual in the network can generate income for not only themselves, but also for the individuals they have recruited.

The Benefits of Network Marketing:

There are several benefits to network marketing, both for the individuals involved in the business and for the companies that use this model. For individuals, network marketing offers a flexible and low-cost way to start their own business. They have the freedom to work from home, set their own schedule, and have control over their earnings. Additionally, network marketers have the opportunity to build a residual income, as they earn not only from their own sales but also from the sales made by the individuals they have recruited.

For companies, network marketing allows them to reach new markets and customers through the efforts of their network marketers. This can result in lower marketing and advertising costs, as well as increased product exposure and brand awareness.

The Potential Earnings in Network Marketing:

The potential earnings in network marketing can vary greatly depending on several factors, such as the amount of time and effort put into the business, the individual's sales and recruiting skills, and the company's compensation plan. However, many network marketers are able to achieve substantial residual income and even reach financial freedom through their network marketing business.

In conclusion, network marketing is a business model that offers individuals the opportunity to start their own business and achieve financial success, while also benefiting companies by allowing them to reach new markets and customers. Understanding the basics of network marketing is the first step in determining if this business model is a good fit for you and your goals.

Network marketing, also known as multi-level marketing (MLM), is a business model that has been gaining popularity in recent years. It is a way of selling products and services through a network of independent distributors, also known as network marketers.

There are many benefits to this business model, including flexibility, low start-up costs, and the potential to earn a residual income. In this chapter, we will explore the top benefits of network marketing and why it may be a great opportunity for those looking to start a business or supplement their income.

Flexibility
One of the biggest benefits of network marketing is the flexibility it offers. Network marketers can work from anywhere and at any time, making it ideal for those who want to start a business but also have other commitments such as a full-time job or family.

Low start-up costs
Starting a traditional business can be expensive, but with network marketing, the start-up costs are much lower. In most cases, the only investment required is the cost of the product kit, which can range from a few hundred dollars to a few thousand dollars. This makes network marketing a great option for those who are just starting out and don't have a lot of capital to invest.

Residual income

Another big benefit of network marketing is the potential to earn a residual income. This means that you will continue to earn income even after the initial sale has been made. This can provide a great source of passive income and can help you reach your financial goals faster.

Personal growth and development

Network marketing also provides the opportunity for personal growth and development. You will have the opportunity to learn new skills, such as sales and marketing, and to develop new relationships with other network marketers. This can help you grow as a person and achieve success both in your personal and professional life.

Unlimited earning potential

The earning potential in network marketing is unlimited, making it a great opportunity for those who want to achieve financial freedom. With the right attitude, dedication, and effort, network marketers can earn a significant income, and even reach six or seven figures over time.

In conclusion, network marketing offers many benefits and is a great opportunity for those who are looking for a flexible business model with low start-up costs and unlimited earning potential. Whether you are just starting out or are looking to supplement your income, network marketing may be the right choice for you.

CHAPTER 12. FINDING THE RIGHT NETWORK MARKETING COMPANY

Starting a network marketing business can be a fantastic opportunity to generate income while also helping others to achieve their own financial goals. However, it is important to choose the right company in order to maximize your chances of success. In this chapter, we will guide you through the key factors to consider when researching a network marketing company, including the company itself, the products and services they offer, and the compensation plan. We will also discuss the key ingredients for building a successful network marketing business, such as building a strong team, staying consistent and dedicated, and continuously learning and growing. By the end of this chapter, you will have a clear understanding of how to evaluate a network marketing company and determine if it is the right fit for you.

Researching the Company

When it comes to finding the right network marketing company, researching the company is an essential step. In this chapter, we will look at what to consider when researching network marketing companies and how to go about finding the right one for you.

The first step in researching a network marketing company is to check its credibility. You want to make sure that the company has a good reputation, is financially stable, and has been in business for a while. You can do this by looking up the company on the Better Business Bureau website and checking if they have any negative reviews or complaints. Additionally, you can look at the company's website and see if they have a history of success and a strong track record.

Next, you want to consider the products and services offered by the company. Make sure that the products are high quality and in demand. Look at the company's sales numbers and see if they are consistently growing. Additionally, research the competition and see how the company's products stack up against them.

It's also important to evaluate the compensation plan offered by the company. Make sure that the plan is fair, transparent, and provides a good return on investment. You can do this by speaking to current members of the network marketing team, researching online and reading reviews, and reaching out to the company's customer support team to ask any questions you may have. In order to make an informed decision, you'll want to understand the company's structure, leadership, and overall financial stability. This information can be found through public filings, industry reports, and the company's own website and promotional materials.

It's also important to consider the products or services that the company offers. Is the product unique, in demand, and of high quality? Are there any competitors offering similar products? Is the company invested in research and development to improve and expand their product line? The answers to these questions can give you insight into the company's focus and commitment to providing value to its customers and members.

Remember, the success of your network marketing business is heavily dependent on the company you choose to partner with. Take the time to thoroughly research the company, understand its compensation plan, and evaluate its products and services before making a commitment. This will help you make an informed decision and increase your chances of building a successful network marketing business.

Understanding the Products and Services

Before you decide to join a network marketing company, it's crucial to understand the products and services that the company offers. In this chapter, we will explore the key factors you need to consider when evaluating a company's products and services.

First, consider the quality of the products and services. Are they of high quality, or do they have a reputation for being low quality? This is important because if the products are of poor quality, it will be difficult to sell them, and you will not be able to build a successful network marketing business.

Second, consider the market demand for the products and services. Are the products and services in demand in the market, or are they niche products that only appeal to a small audience? This is important because if the products are in high demand, it will be easier to sell them and build a successful network marketing business.

Third, consider the price point of the products and services. Are they priced competitively, or are they overpriced compared to similar products in the market? This is important because if the products are priced too high, it will be difficult to sell them and build a successful network marketing business.

Finally, consider the support and resources provided by the company to help you sell the products and services. Are they providing adequate training, marketing materials, and support to help you succeed? This is important because if you do not have the resources and support you need to succeed, it will be difficult to build a successful network marketing business.

In conclusion, when evaluating the products and services offered by a network marketing company, it's crucial to consider the quality, demand, price, and support provided. By taking the time to evaluate these key factors, you can ensure that you are joining a company that offers high-quality products and services that are in demand, priced competitively, and provide the support and resources you need to succeed.

Evaluating the Compensation Plan

One of the most important aspects of finding the right network marketing company is evaluating their compensation plan. The compensation plan determines how you will be paid for your efforts and how much money you can make. It is crucial to understand the compensation plan before joining a network marketing company. In this chapter, we will explore how to evaluate a compensation plan and what to look for.

What is a compensation plan?
A compensation plan is a system that rewards network marketers for selling products and building a team. The plan outlines how you will be paid for your efforts, including bonuses, commissions, and incentives. There are different types of compensation plans, each with its own unique structure.

What to look for in a compensation plan?
When evaluating a compensation plan, it's important to consider the following:

Fairness: Is the compensation plan fair and balanced? Does it provide a good return on investment?

Transparency: Is the compensation plan transparent and easy to understand? Are there any hidden fees or charges?

Earnings potential: What is the potential earnings for network marketers? Can you earn a significant income with the compensation plan?

Bonuses and incentives: Does the company offer bonuses and incentives for reaching certain goals? How often are bonuses paid?

Support and training: Does the company provide support and training to help network marketers succeed?

Long-term sustainability: Is the compensation plan sustainable for the long term? Will it continue to provide a good return on investment in the future?

Once you have evaluated the compensation plan, it's important to ask yourself whether it aligns with your goals and expectations. If the compensation plan meets your standards, it may be a good fit for you. However, if the compensation plan does not meet your standards, it's important to continue your search for a company that does.

In conclusion, evaluating the compensation plan is a crucial step in finding the right network marketing company. By considering the fairness, transparency, earnings potential, and other key factors, you can make an informed decision and find a company that aligns with your goals and expectations.

Building a Successful Network Marketing Business

Building a successful network marketing business requires a combination of effort, dedication, and strategy. In this chapter, we'll take a look at the steps you can take to build a successful network marketing business and achieve your financial goals.

Create a clear business plan: Your business plan should include your goals, target market, and strategies for reaching your target market. It should also outline the steps you will take to reach your goals and how you will measure your progress along the way.

Build a strong team: Building a strong team is crucial for success in network marketing. Look for team members who are passionate about the products and services offered by the company, as well as those who have a strong work ethic and are committed to their own success.

Offer high-quality products and services: Your success in network marketing will depend, in part, on the quality of the products and services you offer. Make sure you have a thorough understanding of the products and services offered by the company, and that you are confident in their quality and value.

Develop strong relationships: Network marketing is all about building relationships. Take the time to get to know your team members, customers, and prospects, and strive to provide them with excellent service and support.

Stay organized: Keep track of your progress and stay organized by using tools such as calendars, to-do lists, and productivity apps. This will help you stay on track and ensure that you are making the most of your time and resources.

Continuously educate yourself: Success in network marketing requires continuous learning and growth. Stay up-to-date on the latest industry trends and strategies, and invest in your own personal development by attending trainings and conferences.

By following these steps, you can build a successful network marketing business that is both profitable and fulfilling. Remember, success in network marketing takes time, effort, and dedication, but with the right approach, you can achieve your financial goals and create a business that you are proud of.

Template for Creating a Successful Network Marketing Business

Start with a clear understanding of the company's products and services, and the target market you want to reach.

Identify your unique selling proposition and how you can differentiate yourself from others in your network.

Create a marketing plan that includes a mix of traditional and digital marketing tactics to reach your target audience.

Utilize the resources provided by the network marketing company to help you build your business, including training, tools, and support from experienced network marketers.

Set achievable and realistic goals for your business and track your progress regularly to make sure you are on the right track.

Focus on building and nurturing relationships with your customers and team members to create a supportive and thriving network.

Continuously learn and grow your business by taking advantage of training and development opportunities, attending events, and networking with other network marketers.

Stay consistent and dedicated to your business, even during tough times, to ensure long-term success.

By following these steps and utilizing the support and resources available to you, you can build a successful network marketing business and reach your financial and personal goals.

Building a Strong Team

Building a strong team is crucial for success in network marketing. Having a team of motivated and dedicated individuals can help you achieve your goals faster and with less effort. Here are some tips for building a strong team in network marketing:

Hire based on culture fit: Make sure that each member of your team shares the same values and vision as you. This will ensure that everyone is working towards the same goal and is dedicated to the success of the team.

Provide training and support: Invest in the training and support of your team members. This will help them to develop the skills they need to succeed in network marketing and increase their confidence in the business.

Encourage collaboration: Foster a culture of collaboration within your team. Encourage open communication and teamwork to ensure that everyone is working together effectively.

Offer incentives: Offer incentives to your team members for their hard work and dedication. This can be in the form of bonuses, recognition, or opportunities for advancement.

Lead by example: Lead by example and show your team members what it takes to succeed in network marketing. Demonstrate the importance of hard work, determination, and a positive attitude.

Stay organized: Keep your team organized by using tools and systems to track their progress and communicate effectively. This will help everyone to stay on the same page and work towards the same goal.

Building a strong team is essential for success in network marketing. By following these tips, you can create a team of motivated and dedicated individuals who will help you achieve your goals and grow your business.

Staying Consistent and Dedicated

Building a successful network marketing business requires dedication, hard work, and consistency. It's easy to get caught up in the excitement of starting a new venture and lose focus along the way. However, staying consistent and dedicated to your goals is essential to achieving success in network marketing.

Here are a few tips for staying consistent and dedicated to your network marketing business:

Set clear goals: Have a clear understanding of what you want to achieve, and set specific and measurable goals to track your progress. This will help you stay focused and motivated.

Make a plan: Develop a detailed plan for how you will achieve your goals. This plan should include the steps you need to take, the resources you need, and the timeline for achieving each goal.

Stay organized: Organize your time and resources to maximize your efficiency and productivity. Keep a schedule, set reminders, and prioritize your tasks to ensure that you stay on track.

Surround yourself with support: Surround yourself with supportive people who believe in your vision and are willing to help you succeed. This can include friends, family, business partners, and even online communities.

Stay positive: Stay positive and maintain a growth mindset. Network marketing is a journey, and it's important to stay optimistic and focused on your goals even when faced with challenges.

Celebrate your successes: Take time to celebrate your successes and acknowledge your progress. This will help you stay motivated and focused on your goals.

Continuous learning: Network marketing is a dynamic industry, and it's important to stay current and informed. Continuously learn and grow your skills and knowledge to stay ahead of the competition.

By staying consistent and dedicated to your network marketing business, you will increase your chances of success and achieve your goals more quickly. Remember to take things one step at a time, stay organized, and seek out support and guidance from others as needed.

Continuously Learning and Growing

The network marketing industry is constantly evolving, and it's important to stay informed about the latest trends and best practices. This will help you stay ahead of the competition and continue to grow your business. To achieve success in network marketing, you must be a lifelong learner who is always looking for ways to improve.

Here are some tips for continuously learning and growing in the network marketing industry:

Attend workshops, conferences, and webinars: These events are a great way to stay up-to-date on the latest trends and best practices in network marketing. They provide a platform to connect with other network marketers, learn from industry leaders, and gain new insights.

Read books and articles: There are many great resources available for network marketers, including books and articles written by industry experts. Take advantage of these resources to learn about new strategies and techniques, and stay informed about industry trends.

Join online communities: Participating in online communities, such as Facebook groups, can be a great way to connect with other network marketers, share ideas, and learn from others. You can also ask questions, share your experiences, and receive feedback from other professionals.

Partner with a mentor: Working with a mentor can be an invaluable experience for network marketers. A mentor can provide guidance, support, and help you avoid common mistakes. Find a mentor who has experience in your niche and is willing to share their knowledge and insights.

Experiment and test new ideas: One of the best ways to learn is by experimenting and testing new ideas. This will help you stay innovative, and identify what works and what doesn't work in your business.

In conclusion, the key to success in network marketing is to be a continuous learner. By staying informed, connecting with other network marketers, and continuously experimenting and testing new ideas, you can ensure that your business continues to grow and thrive.

PART 3
ADVANCED TOPICS

CHAPTER 13: BUILDING A SALES FUNNEL

Introduction to Sales Funnels

In today's fast-paced digital world, a sales funnel is an essential tool for any business looking to grow and succeed. A sales funnel is a step-by-step process that guides your prospects through the journey of becoming a customer, starting from the moment they first become aware of your brand to the moment they make a purchase.

A well-designed sales funnel can help you maximize the value of each customer and increase your conversion rates, which in turn will lead to more sales and higher profits. This chapter will provide an introduction to the basics of sales funnels and help you understand the key elements that make them work.

Types of Sales Funnels

There are many different types of sales funnels, each with its own unique benefits and challenges. Some of the most common types of sales funnels include the Awareness Funnel, the Interest Funnel, the Desire Funnel, and the Action Funnel.

Each type of sales funnel serves a specific purpose and is designed to target a different stage of the customer journey. Understanding these different types of funnels and how they work is crucial to developing a successful sales strategy.

A sales funnel is a step-by-step process that guides potential customers from initial awareness of your product or service to making a purchase. The purpose of a sales funnel is to turn a stranger into a customer and then into a repeat buyer. There are several types of sales funnels, each with its own set of advantages and disadvantages. In this chapter, we will explore the different types of sales funnels and help you determine which one is right for your business.

Awareness Funnel

The Awareness Funnel is the first stage in the sales funnel process. This funnel is designed to create awareness of your product or service and educate potential customers about its features and benefits. The goal of this funnel is to generate leads and build your email list. To do this, you can use tactics such as blog posts, videos, social media, and webinars to educate your audience and attract them to your website.

Interest Funnel

The Interest Funnel is the second stage in the sales funnel process. This funnel is designed to capture the attention of your leads and turn them into paying customers. The goal of this funnel is to build trust and establish a relationship with your audience. To do this, you can offer free trials, demos, or samples of your product or service. You can also use email marketing, retargeting ads, and webinars to continue to educate your audience and build trust.

Desire Funnel

The Desire Funnel is the third stage in the sales funnel process. This funnel is designed to create a sense of urgency and a strong desire for your product or service. The goal of this funnel is to get your leads to make a purchase. To do this, you can use limited-time offers, scarcity tactics, and social proof to increase the perceived value of your product or service.

Action Funnel

The Action Funnel is the fourth and final stage in the sales funnel process. This funnel is designed to convert your leads into paying customers. The goal of this funnel is to make the sale and provide a great customer experience. To do this, you can use a checkout page, order form, or other conversion optimization tactics to make it easy for your leads to make a purchase.

By understanding the different types of sales funnels, you can design a sales funnel that will help you turn strangers into customers and grow your business. In the next chapter, we will explore how to design your sales funnel to maximize results and conversion rates.

Designing Your Sales Funnel

Designing your sales funnel is the first step in creating a successful marketing campaign. This process involves identifying your target audience, mapping out their journey from awareness to purchase, and choosing the best type of funnel to reach your goals.

It's important to keep in mind that your sales funnel should be optimized for conversion, which means it should be simple, easy to use, and provide a clear call to action at each stage. Your sales funnel should also be optimized for the devices and platforms your target audience is most likely to use.

Step by Step in Understanding the Design in Your Sales Funnel

A sales funnel is the process through which a potential customer is taken from initial awareness to final purchase. It is a crucial component of any successful marketing strategy. When designed properly, a sales funnel can help you convert more prospects into customers and increase your overall revenue. In this chapter, we will take a closer look at the key elements of a well-designed sales funnel.

The first step in designing your sales funnel is to determine your target audience. Who are the people that you want to reach with your marketing message? What are their needs, desires, and pain points? Understanding your target audience will help you create a sales funnel that resonates with them and guides them towards a purchase.

Once you have a clear understanding of your target audience, it's time to map out the stages of your sales funnel. A typical sales funnel includes the following stages:

Awareness: In this stage, you introduce your target audience to your brand and your products or services. Your goal is to create interest and generate leads.

Interest: In this stage, you deepen your target audience's engagement with your brand by providing them with valuable information and offering them something of value.

Decision: In this stage, you present your offer and help your target audience make a decision to purchase.

Action: In this stage, you close the sale by guiding your target audience through the purchasing process.

It's important to remember that each stage of your sales funnel should be designed to build on the previous one. The goal is to take your target audience on a journey that ultimately leads them to make a purchase.

To design a successful sales funnel, you will need to consider the following elements:

Landing pages: A landing page is a specific web page that a potential customer lands on after clicking a link. Your landing pages should be optimized for conversion and should clearly communicate the next step in your sales funnel.

Lead magnets: A lead magnet is a valuable resource or incentive that you offer in exchange for a potential customer's contact information. Lead magnets can be anything from a free trial or demo to an e-book or course.

Calls to action: A call to action (CTA) is a button or link that encourages your target audience to take a specific action, such as making a purchase or downloading a lead magnet. Your CTAs should be clear and prominent throughout your sales funnel.

Email sequences: Email sequences are a series of automated emails that are triggered by a specific action, such as signing up for a lead magnet. Email sequences can help you build rapport with your target audience, provide them with valuable information, and guide them towards a purchase.

Upsells and downsells: Upsells and downsells are offers for complementary or alternative products that are presented to a customer after they have made a purchase. Upsells and downsells can help increase the value of each customer's purchase and boost your overall revenue.

By following these best practices for designing your sales funnel, you can create a process that is optimized for conversion and helps you build strong relationships with your target audience. But the process doesn't end there. You must continuously test and optimize your sales funnel to ensure that it is delivering the results that you want. In the next chapter, we will explore the importance of testing and optimizing your sales funnel to yield great results.

Testing and Optimizing Your Sales Funnel

A sales funnel is an essential tool for converting leads into paying customers. However, simply having a sales funnel in place is not enough to ensure success. To maximize the impact and effectiveness of your sales funnel, it's crucial to regularly test and optimize it. This chapter will discuss the importance of testing and optimization in the sales funnel process and provide tips on how to effectively implement these processes.

The Importance of Testing and Optimization

Testing and optimization are ongoing processes that help you refine your sales funnel to ensure that it's delivering the best results possible. By regularly testing and refining your sales funnel, you can identify areas that need improvement and make the necessary changes to maximize its impact and effectiveness. This is essential to the success of your marketing strategy, as even small changes can have a big impact on your conversion rate.

What to Test

When testing your sales funnel, it's important to focus on elements that have a significant impact on conversion rates, such as the copy, design, and call to action. You may also want to test other elements, such as the pricing of your products or services, the delivery methods, and the follow-up process.

Copy Testing

The copy used in your sales funnel is one of the most important elements to test. It should be clear, concise, and communicate the value of your products or services effectively. To test your copy, try using different wording or phrasing, or even different headlines, to see what resonates best with your audience.

Design Testing

The design of your sales funnel is another important aspect to test. A well-designed sales funnel should be visually appealing, easy to navigate, and provide a clear path to conversion. To test your design, try different layouts, colors, and images to see what resonates best with your audience.

Call to Action Testing

The call to action (CTA) is the button or link that encourages visitors to take the desired action, such as making a purchase or filling out a form. It's important to test different CTAs to see what works best for your audience. You may want to try different wording, colors, and placement to see what resonates best.

How to Test

There are several methods for testing your sales funnel, including A/B testing and multivariate testing. A/B testing involves creating two versions of the same page and testing each version to see which one performs better. Multivariate testing involves testing multiple elements at the same time to see which combination of elements produces the best results.

Regardless of the method you choose, it's important to gather data on your results and use it to make informed decisions. This may involve tracking the conversion rate, engagement rate, and bounce rate of your sales funnel, among other metrics.

Optimizing Your Sales Funnel

Once you have gathered data from your tests, it's time to optimize your sales funnel. This may involve making changes to the copy, design, and call to action, as well as other elements that were found to be ineffective during testing.

It's important to continue testing and optimizing your sales funnel on an ongoing basis to ensure that it's delivering the best results possible. This may involve trying new tactics, such as changing the lead magnet or offering a special promotion, to see what works best for your audience.

Testing and optimization are crucial to the success of your sales funnel. By regularly testing and refining your sales funnel, you can identify areas that need improvement and make the necessary changes to maximize its impact and effectiveness. By continuously testing and optimizing your sales funnel, you can stay ahead of the competition and ensure that you are delivering the best possible experience to your audience.

There are a variety of tests that you can perform on your sales funnel to determine what is working and what is not. For example, you might test different headlines or images to see which ones generate the most engagement. You could also test different pricing structures to see what drives the most conversions.

Once you have conducted your tests, it's important to analyze the results and make data-driven decisions about what changes to make. This might involve adjusting your copy, changing your pricing strategy, or making other modifications to improve the performance of your sales funnel.

It's also important to track your results over time to see if your changes are having the desired effect. By continuously monitoring your sales funnel, you can quickly identify any issues and make adjustments as needed to keep it running smoothly.

In conclusion, testing and optimizing your sales funnel is an ongoing process that requires dedication and commitment. By regularly testing and refining your funnel, you can ensure that it is delivering the best possible results and helping you achieve your business goals.

CHAPTER 14: CREATING LANDING PAGES

Introduction to Landing Pages
Designing an Effective Landing Page
Elements of a High-Converting Landing Page
A/B Testing Your Landing Pages

Landing pages play a crucial role in the success of your marketing campaigns. They are the first point of contact between your potential customers and your brand, and as such, it's essential to make sure they are designed effectively. In this chapter, we'll be exploring the basics of landing pages, including what they are, why they're important, and how to design an effective landing page.

We'll also be discussing the key elements of a high-converting landing page, and how to use A/B testing to optimize your landing pages and improve their performance. Whether you're a seasoned marketer or just starting out, this chapter will provide you with the knowledge and tools you need to create landing pages that convert visitors into customers.

Designing an Effective Landing Page

When it comes to marketing, your landing page is often the first point of contact between your business and potential customers. It's critical that your landing page effectively communicates your value proposition and converts visitors into customers.

The design of your landing page plays a crucial role in its success. An effective landing page should be visually appealing, easy to navigate, and deliver a clear and concise message. Here are some key elements to consider when designing your landing page:

A clear and compelling headline: Your headline should immediately grab the attention of your visitors and clearly state the purpose of your landing page.

A strong value proposition: Clearly state the unique value that your business offers and why your product or service is better than the competition.

A focused call to action: Encourage visitors to take a specific action, such as signing up for a free trial or making a purchase.

Engaging visuals: Use high-quality images and videos to help communicate your message and engage your visitors.

Easy navigation: Make sure that your landing page is easy to navigate, with a clear structure and intuitive navigation menu.

Mobile optimization: With an increasing number of people browsing the web on their mobile devices, it's important that your landing page is optimized for mobile viewing.

By considering these key elements, you can design an effective landing page that effectively communicates your value proposition and converts visitors into customers. A well-designed landing page is a critical component of any successful marketing campaign, so take the time to get it right.

Elements of a High-Converting Landing Page

When it comes to marketing, your landing page is often the first point of contact between your business and potential customers. It's critical that your landing page effectively communicates your value proposition and converts visitors into customers.

The design of your landing page plays a crucial role in its success. An effective landing page should be visually appealing, easy to navigate, and deliver a clear and concise message. Here are some key elements to consider when designing your landing page:

A clear and compelling headline: Your headline should immediately grab the attention of your visitors and clearly state the purpose of your landing page.

A strong value proposition: Clearly state the unique value that your business offers and why your product or service is better than the competition.

A focused call to action: Encourage visitors to take a specific action, such as signing up for a free trial or making a purchase.

Engaging visuals: Use high-quality images and videos to help communicate your message and engage your visitors.

Easy navigation: Make sure that your landing page is easy to navigate, with a clear structure and intuitive navigation menu.

Mobile optimization: With an increasing number of people browsing the web on their mobile devices, it's important that your landing page is optimized for mobile viewing.

By considering these key elements, you can design an effective landing page that effectively communicates your value proposition and converts visitors into customers. A well-designed landing page is a critical component of any successful marketing campaign, so take the time to get it right.

A/B Testing Your Landing Pages

A/B testing, also known as split testing, is a critical component of effective landing page design. It involves creating two versions of your landing page and comparing the performance of each to determine which version delivers the best results. This process can help you identify what elements of your landing page are working well and which need improvement, allowing you to make data-driven decisions to optimize your page for maximum conversion rates.

Before beginning your A/B testing, it's important to determine what you want to test. Common elements to test include the headline, images, layout, call to action, and color scheme. Start by testing one element at a time so you can easily identify the impact of each change.

Once you have decided what to test, you can use a landing page optimization tool to split your visitors between the two versions of your page and track the results. The tool will then automatically redirect visitors to the version of the page that performs the best.

It's important to note that A/B testing requires patience. The results may not be immediate, and it may take several rounds of testing to see significant results. Be sure to track your results over time and continually make changes based on the data you receive.

A/B testing is an ongoing process that should be part of your overall marketing strategy. By continually testing and optimizing your landing pages, you can stay ahead of the competition and increase your conversion rates, leading to more sales and revenue for your business.

In conclusion, creating effective landing pages is an essential part of any affiliate marketing or digital marketing strategy. By understanding the key elements of a high-converting landing page and regularly testing and optimizing your pages, you can maximize their impact and effectiveness.

The process of designing and testing landing pages is ongoing and requires dedication and attention to detail. However, with the right approach, you can create landing pages that drive results, increase conversions, and grow your business.

So, take the time to research, understand, and implement the key elements of a high-converting landing page. With the right approach, you can see significant results from your landing pages and take your business to the next level.

CHAPTER 15: COPYWRITING TECHNIQUES

Introduction to Copywriting
 Understanding Your Target Audience
Writing Headlines That Convert
 Crafting a Strong Value Proposition
 Writing Convincing Body Copy
 Optimizing Your Copy for Conversions

Introduction to Copywriting

Copywriting is the art of creating persuasive, compelling, and engaging written content that convinces your target audience to take action. Whether it's to make a purchase, sign up for a newsletter, or complete a form, copywriting plays a crucial role in the success of your marketing efforts.

Understanding Your Target Audience

Copywriting is a powerful tool in marketing, and it's essential to get it right. One of the most crucial aspects of copywriting is understanding your target audience. Your target audience is the group of people who you are trying to reach with your marketing messages, and it's important to have a clear understanding of who they are, what they need, and what motivates them.

Why Understanding Your Target Audience is Important

Understanding your target audience is critical for creating successful marketing campaigns and building strong relationships with your customers. By knowing who your target audience is, you can create messages and offers that resonate with them and meet their needs. This will help you build trust and credibility with your audience and increase conversions.

Identifying Your Target Audience

The first step in understanding your target audience is to identify who they are. This can involve researching demographics such as age, gender, education level, income, and location, as well as psychographic information such as interests, values, and attitudes. This information can be obtained through surveys, focus groups, or analysis of your existing customer data.

Understanding Their Needs, Wants, Pain Points, and Goals

Once you have identified your target audience, it's important to understand their needs, wants, pain points, and goals. This will help you create copy that speaks directly to them and addresses their specific needs and wants. For example, if your target audience is busy professionals, your copy might focus on the convenience and time-saving benefits of your product or service.

What Motivates Them to Take Action

Finally, it's essential to understand what motivates your target audience to take action. This could be a desire for a better life, a need to solve a problem, or a fear of missing out on a valuable opportunity. Understanding what motivates your target audience will help you craft copy that appeals to their emotions and drives action.

In conclusion, understanding your target audience is a crucial aspect of effective copywriting. By knowing who your target audience is, what they need, and what motivates them, you can create copy that resonates with them and drives results.

Writing Headlines That Convert

A headline is the first thing your audience will see and it's often what determines whether they will continue reading your copy or move on. A great headline has the power to grab the reader's attention, create interest, and convince them to take action.

Here are some tips for writing headlines that convert:

Be Clear and Direct: The headline should clearly communicate the main benefit of your offer and what the reader can expect if they continue reading.

Make it Urgent: Creating a sense of urgency can help to motivate readers to take action. This can be done by using words like "limited time only", "act now", or "limited spots available".

Use Active Voice: Writing headlines in active voice, rather than passive voice, makes them more impactful and engaging.

Keep it Short: Keep your headlines short and to the point, ideally around 10-15 words or less. This makes it easier for the reader to quickly understand what your offer is about.

Test and Refine: A/B test your headlines to see which ones perform best. This will help you identify what works and what doesn't, allowing you to refine and optimize your headlines over time.

Writing headlines that convert is an important part of copywriting and a crucial step in creating a successful sales funnel. By using these tips, you can create headlines that grab the reader's attention, create interest, and motivate them to take action.

Crafting a Strong Value Proposition

Introduction

Your value proposition is the cornerstone of your marketing strategy and a critical component of your sales funnel. It's the promise you make to your target audience about the benefits they will receive from your product or service. Your value proposition should be clear, concise, and persuasive, and it should convince your target audience to take action.

What is a Value Proposition?

A value proposition is a clear statement that defines what sets you apart from your competition and why your target audience should choose your product or service over others. It should highlight the benefits that your product or service provides, and why it's unique and different from what's already on the market. Your value proposition should also demonstrate how your product or service will solve your target audience's needs, wants, or pain points.

Importance of a Strong Value Proposition

A strong value proposition is essential for the success of your business. It helps you stand out from your competition and communicates the unique benefits of your product or service. It also helps you attract and retain customers, as it demonstrates how your product or service can solve their needs and wants. A strong value proposition is a key component of your marketing strategy, as it helps you differentiate your business and create a compelling reason for customers to choose you over your competition.

How to Craft a Strong Value Proposition

Crafting a strong value proposition requires you to understand your target audience, as well as your competition. You should start by researching your target audience and identifying their needs, wants, pain points, and goals. This will help you understand what motivates them to take action and what they're looking for in a product or service.

Next, you should research your competition and identify their strengths and weaknesses. This will help you understand what sets you apart from your competition and what makes your product or service unique.

Once you have this information, you can start crafting your value proposition. Your value proposition should be clear, concise, and persuasive, and it should communicate the unique benefits of your product or service. It should also demonstrate how your product or service solves your target audience's needs, wants, or pain points.

Tips for Crafting a Strong Value Proposition

Here are some tips to help you craft a strong value proposition:

Keep it simple and clear: Your value proposition should be easy to understand and straightforward. It should clearly communicate the benefits of your product or service and why it's unique.

Make it specific: Your value proposition should be specific and targeted to your target audience. It should demonstrate how your product or service solves their needs, wants, or pain points.

Make it memorable: Your value proposition should be memorable and stick in the minds of your target audience. It should be easy to recall and memorable.

Make it unique: Your value proposition should set you apart from your competition and demonstrate what makes your product or service unique.

Make it credible: Your value proposition should be credible and demonstrate why your product or service is the best solution for your target audience.

Conclusion

Crafting a strong value proposition is essential for the success of your business. It helps you stand out from your competition and communicates the unique benefits of your product or service. By understanding your target audience and researching your competition, you can craft a value proposition that resonates with your target audience and drives results. Remember, your value proposition should be clear, concise, and persuasive, and it should communicate the unique benefits of your product or service.

Writing Convincing Body Copy

The body copy is a critical component of your sales funnel and is the section of your landing page where you expand on your value proposition and provide additional details about your offer. The goal of the body copy is to engage and persuade your target audience to take action.

Here are some tips for writing convincing body copy:

Keep it simple and easy to read: Use short paragraphs, bullet points, and subheadings to break up the text and make it easier for your audience to read and understand.

Focus on benefits: Highlight the benefits of your offer, rather than just the features. Explain how your product or service will improve the lives of your target audience and what they can expect to gain from using it.

Address common objections: Anticipate the objections that your target audience may have and address them directly in the body copy. This will help to build trust and credibility, and increase the chances of them taking action.

Use stories and case studies: People are more likely to remember stories and real-life examples, so use them to illustrate your points and make your offer more relatable.

Create a sense of urgency: Encourage your target audience to take action now, rather than later. Use language that creates a sense of urgency, such as "limited time only" or "while stocks last".

Keep it concise: Avoid using filler words and phrases, and stick to the facts. Your body copy should be concise, yet persuasive, and focused on driving your target audience towards the desired action.

By following these tips, you can write body copy that is convincing, engaging, and effective in driving conversions. Remember to keep testing and refining your copy as needed, to ensure that it is delivering the best results possible.

Optimizing Your Copy for Conversions

Introduction to Optimizing Your Copy for Conversions

Copywriting is an art and a science, and it's essential to optimize your copy to get the best results possible. Optimizing your copy involves continuously testing and refining your copy to improve its impact and effectiveness. The goal is to increase your conversion rates and achieve better results.

Testing and Refining Your Copy

To optimize your copy for conversions, it's essential to regularly test and refine it. This may involve testing different headlines, calls to action, or body copy to see what works best. You can use tools such as A/B testing to compare different versions of your copy and determine which one is most effective.

A/B testing is a powerful tool that allows you to compare two versions of your copy side by side to see which one performs better. You can test different elements of your copy, such as headlines, calls to action, or body copy, to see what resonates best with your target audience.

One important factor to keep in mind when optimizing your copy is to test only one element at a time. This will help you determine which changes are driving the results and avoid overcomplicating the process.

Data-Driven Decision Making

When optimizing your copy, it's crucial to base your decisions on data. Use analytics and tracking tools to monitor your copy's performance and make data-driven decisions. This will help you understand what's working and what's not, and it will allow you to make the necessary changes to improve your results.

Continuously Evaluate and Refine

Optimizing your copy is an ongoing process, and it's essential to continuously evaluate and refine it. Regularly test and refine your copy to ensure that it is delivering the best results possible. This will help you stay ahead of the competition and achieve better results over time.

Conclusion

Optimizing your copy for conversions is an essential part of any successful marketing strategy. By regularly testing and refining your copy, you can identify areas that need improvement and make the necessary changes to maximize its impact and effectiveness. Continuously optimizing your copy will help you increase your conversion rates and achieve better results.

CHAPTER 16: DEVELOPING AN AFFILIATE MARKETING STRATEGY

Introduction to Affiliate Marketing
Defining Your Niche
Finding the Right Products to Promote
Building a Network of Affiliates
Tracking and Optimizing Your Affiliate Campaigns

Introduction to Affiliate Marketing

Affiliate marketing is a performance-based marketing model that allows businesses to promote their products through affiliates, who receive a commission for each sale they generate. As an affiliate marketer, your goal is to promote products that are relevant to your target audience and generate sales, while also building a profitable business.

Defining Your Niche

Defining your niche is a crucial step in the affiliate marketing process. By identifying your target audience and the products they are interested in, you can develop a focused and effective marketing strategy. This will help you stand out from the competition and attract the right customers to your offer.

Your niche should be based on your personal interests, expertise, and passions, as well as the needs and wants of your target audience. You can research your target audience by looking at demographic information, such as age, gender, location, and income, as well as their pain points, goals, and motivators.

Once you have a clear understanding of your target audience, you can select products that are relevant to them and that will appeal to their needs and wants. This could be products related to your personal interests and passions, or it could be products that address specific pain points or challenges that your target audience is facing.

By defining your niche, you can develop a marketing strategy that is tailored to your target audience, and that will help you reach your ideal customers effectively. This will increase your chances of success in affiliate marketing and allow you to achieve better results.

Finding the Right Products to Promote

Finding the right products to promote as an affiliate marketer is crucial to the success of your affiliate marketing strategy. Not only do you want to choose products that align with your niche and target audience, but you also want to select products that have a high demand, a strong value proposition, and a solid reputation in the market.

One way to find the right products to promote is by researching and evaluating different affiliate programs. This can be done through online marketplaces, such as ClickBank and Commission Junction, or by reaching out to individual companies to inquire about their affiliate programs.

When evaluating potential products to promote, consider factors such as commission rate, product popularity, and customer reviews. It is also important to try out the products yourself to ensure that they meet your expectations and will provide a positive experience for your customers.

In addition to evaluating individual products, consider the reputation and reliability of the companies behind them. Partnering with reputable companies will not only increase the credibility of your recommendations, but it will also ensure that you receive your commission payments in a timely manner.

Finding the right products to promote takes time and research, but it is an essential step in developing a successful affiliate marketing strategy. By selecting the right products, you can build trust with your target audience and maximize your earnings as an affiliate marketer.

Building a Network of Affiliates

Building a network of affiliates is a key part of an effective affiliate marketing strategy. An affiliate network is a group of individuals or companies that promote your products and earn a commission for each sale they generate. Building a network of affiliates can help you expand your reach, drive more traffic to your website, and increase your sales.

To build a network of affiliates, you can reach out to bloggers, influencers, and other businesses in your niche and offer them a commission for promoting your products. You can also use affiliate marketing networks, such as Commission Junction or Shareasale, to connect with affiliates and manage your affiliate relationships.

When building your affiliate network, it is important to offer competitive commission rates and provide your affiliates with the resources and support they need to succeed. This may include marketing materials, such as banners and product descriptions, as well as tracking and reporting tools to help them track their sales and commissions.

Having a strong network of affiliates is essential to the success of your affiliate marketing program, so it is important to invest time and resources into building and maintaining relationships with your affiliates. By working closely with your affiliates and providing them with the tools and support they need to succeed, you can achieve a successful and profitable affiliate marketing program.

Tracking and Optimizing Your Affiliate Campaigns

As an affiliate marketer, it is crucial to continuously monitor and optimize your campaigns to ensure their success. The process of tracking and optimization allows you to analyze your results, identify areas for improvement, and make necessary changes to achieve better outcomes. In this chapter, we will delve into the steps involved in tracking and optimizing your affiliate campaigns.

The first step in tracking and optimization is to establish key performance indicators (KPIs). These are metrics that are relevant to your business and will give you a clear picture of the performance of your campaigns. Examples of KPIs for affiliate marketing include click-through rate (CTR), conversion rate, average order value, and revenue generated. By setting these KPIs, you will be able to measure the success of your campaigns and track their progress over time.

Once you have established your KPIs, it's time to monitor your campaigns. This involves regularly reviewing your results and comparing them to your KPIs. If you notice any areas of underperformance, it's time to start making changes to your campaigns. This may involve adjusting your target audience, changing your product offerings, or tweaking your copy and messaging.

In addition to monitoring your campaigns, it's important to conduct A/B testing. This involves creating two versions of your campaigns and testing them to see which one performs better. For example, you may test two different headlines, two different product images, or two different calls to action. By continuously conducting A/B testing, you can determine what works best for your target audience and optimize your campaigns accordingly.

Finally, it's important to continually monitor and analyze your data to ensure that your campaigns are delivering the best results possible. This may involve reviewing your affiliate network's analytics, analyzing your conversion rates, or monitoring your social media metrics. By continuously analyzing your data, you can make informed decisions about how to optimize your campaigns and achieve better results.

In conclusion, tracking and optimization are essential components of a successful affiliate marketing strategy. By continuously monitoring your campaigns, conducting A/B testing, and analyzing your data, you can stay ahead of the competition and achieve success in your affiliate marketing business.

CHAPTER 17:
MANAGING TAXES AS AN
AFFILIATE MARKETER

Understanding the Tax Obligations of Affiliate Marketers
  Keeping Accurate Records
  Deducting Business Expenses
  Understanding Withholding and Reporting Requirements
  Seeking Professional Tax Advice.

As an affiliate marketer, it is important to understand your tax obligations and take the necessary steps to ensure that you are in compliance with the laws and regulations. In this chapter, we will explore the various tax considerations that you need to be aware of, including keeping accurate records, deducting business expenses, understanding withholding and reporting requirements, and seeking professional tax advice. Whether you are just starting out or are an experienced affiliate marketer, this chapter will provide you with the information and tools you need to manage your taxes effectively and avoid any potential legal or financial issues.

Understanding the Tax Obligations of Affiliate Marketers

As an affiliate marketer, it is important to understand your tax obligations in order to remain compliant with tax laws and avoid any potential penalties. Tax obligations for affiliate marketers can vary depending on the country and jurisdiction in which they operate. However, in most cases, affiliate marketers are responsible for reporting their income, paying taxes on their earnings, and keeping accurate records of their business expenses.

It is also important to note that affiliate marketing income may be subject to different tax treatments, depending on the specific arrangement between the affiliate and the advertiser. For example, some affiliate marketers may be considered independent contractors while others may be considered employees, which can have different tax implications.

It is important to familiarize yourself with the tax laws in your jurisdiction and consult with a professional tax advisor if you have any questions or concerns. By taking the necessary steps to understand and comply with your tax obligations, you can protect yourself from any potential legal or financial consequences.

Keeping Accurate Records

Keeping accurate records is an essential aspect of managing your taxes as an affiliate marketer. Accurate record-keeping allows you to track your income and expenses, which is essential for determining your tax liability. Additionally, having accurate records can help you avoid any issues with the tax authorities, as well as provide you with a clearer picture of the financial health of your affiliate marketing business.

There are a few key steps you can take to ensure that your records are accurate and up-to-date. Firstly, it is important to set up a system for tracking your income and expenses, such as using an accounting software or a spreadsheet. This will help you keep track of all your financial transactions and ensure that your records are accurate and complete.

Additionally, it is important to keep all receipts and invoices related to your affiliate marketing business. These documents serve as proof of your expenses and income, and can be used to support your claims if necessary. You should store these documents in a safe and accessible place, so that you can easily retrieve them when needed.

Finally, it is important to regularly review and reconcile your records. This will help you identify any errors or discrepancies, and make sure that your records are accurate and complete. By keeping accurate records, you can ensure that you are meeting your tax obligations and avoid any issues with the tax authorities.

Deducting Business Expenses

As an affiliate marketer, it is important to understand the tax implications of your business and to keep accurate records of all your expenses. By tracking and documenting your expenses, you can deduct them from your taxes and reduce your tax liability. Some common business expenses for affiliate marketers include advertising and marketing costs, software and subscription fees, office supplies, and travel expenses related to attending events or networking opportunities.

To deduct business expenses, it is important to keep detailed and accurate records of all your expenditures. This may include receipts, invoices, or other documentation that supports the expense. Additionally, you should ensure that your expenses are directly related to your business and are necessary for the operation of your business.

When documenting your expenses, it is important to categorize them correctly, so that you can easily find the information you need when it is time to file your taxes. You may also want to consider using accounting software or an online expense tracking tool to help you manage your records.

By keeping accurate records and documenting your expenses, you can ensure that you are in compliance with tax laws and take advantage of all the deductions available to you as an affiliate marketer. This can help you to minimize your tax liability and maximize your profitability.

Understanding Withholding and Reporting Requirements

As an affiliate marketer, it is important to understand the withholding and reporting requirements that apply to your business. This includes understanding the taxes that must be paid on the income you earn through affiliate marketing, as well as the deadlines for paying and reporting these taxes. Failure to comply with these requirements can result in penalties, interest, and other consequences, so it is important to stay informed and up-to-date on the latest requirements.

Withholding taxes refer to the taxes that must be paid to the government on a regular basis, usually on a monthly or quarterly basis, in order to meet your tax obligations. These taxes may include federal income tax, state income tax, and self-employment tax. As an affiliate marketer, you are responsible for estimating the amount of taxes you will owe and making the necessary payments to the government.

Reporting requirements refer to the requirement to file tax returns and other reports with the government in order to accurately report your income and tax obligations. This may include filing an annual tax return, a self-employment tax return, and other reports as required by your state and local tax authorities. It is important to stay informed of the latest reporting requirements and to file accurate and complete reports in a timely manner.

In addition to withholding and reporting requirements, it is also important to understand the tax laws and regulations that apply to your business. This may include understanding the deductions and credits available to affiliate marketers, as well as the tax implications of running a home-based business. By staying informed and up-to-date on the latest tax requirements, you can ensure that you comply with all relevant laws and regulations, and avoid any unnecessary tax liabilities.

Seeking Professional Tax Advice

Seeking professional tax advice is an important step for any affiliate marketer who wants to stay compliant with tax laws and regulations. Working with a tax professional can help you navigate the complex tax obligations associated with affiliate marketing, and ensure that you are making the right decisions to minimize your tax liability.

By seeking professional tax advice, you can benefit from the expertise and experience of a tax professional who has a deep understanding of the tax laws and regulations that apply to affiliate marketers. They can help you understand your obligations, determine the right strategies for minimizing your tax liability, and provide guidance on how to properly report your earnings and deductions.

In addition, working with a tax professional can help you stay ahead of changes in tax laws and regulations, and ensure that you are always in compliance with the latest requirements. This can help you avoid costly fines and penalties, and give you peace of mind knowing that you are making the right decisions for your business.

It's important to note that tax laws and regulations can vary by country and state, so it is essential to seek the advice of a tax professional who has experience working with affiliate marketers in your jurisdiction.

In summary, seeking professional tax advice is a smart investment for any affiliate marketer who wants to ensure compliance, minimize tax liability, and achieve financial success in their business.

In conclusion, affiliate marketing can be a lucrative and fulfilling career choice for those who are willing to invest the time and effort to learn the industry and execute a well-planned strategy. This book has covered the key concepts and best practices of affiliate marketing, from finding your niche, to selecting the right products, to developing a marketing plan, to managing taxes.

To become a successful affiliate marketer, it's essential to stay up-to-date with the latest industry trends, and continuously educate yourself on new strategies and techniques. There are many resources available that can help you along your journey, including:

Affiliate marketing forums and communities: These are online groups where you can connect with other affiliate marketers, ask questions, and share your experiences. Some popular forums include the Affiliate Marketing Forum and the Warrior Forum.

Industry blogs and podcasts: There are many blogs and podcasts that cover the latest news and trends in affiliate marketing. Some of the most popular include the Affiliate Marketing Blog, Smart Passive Income, and the Affiliate Buzz podcast.

Affiliate marketing conferences: Attending conferences and events can provide an opportunity to network with other affiliate marketers, learn from industry experts, and stay up-to-date on the latest developments. Some popular conferences include Affiliate Summit, ClickBank Builders, and Affiliate World Asia.

Lead magnets: Lead magnets are free gifts that you can offer in exchange for someone's email address. They are a great way to build your email list and generate leads for your affiliate marketing business. Some popular lead magnets include ebooks, courses, and webinars.

Affiliate networks: Affiliate networks are intermediaries that connect merchants and affiliate marketers. Some of the most popular affiliate networks include ClickBank, Commission Junction, and ShareASale. These networks offer a wide range of products to promote and provide tracking and reporting tools to help you monitor your results.

With the right tools, resources, and mindset, you can build a successful affiliate marketing business and achieve your financial and personal goals. The key is to stay focused, take action, and never stop learning.

www.ingramcontent.com/pod-product-compliance
Lightning Source LLC
Chambersburg PA
CBHW040926210326
41597CB00030B/5188